Liberty&Learning

THE ESSENTIAL JAMES MADISON

BY

PHILIP BIGLER

Director of the James Madison Center

WITH

ANNIE LORSBACH

Director of Historical Research

&

SHAY COCHRANE

Photo Editor

THE JAMES MADISON CENTER

James Madison University

Harrisonburg, Virginia

THE JAMES MADISON CENTER
James Madison University

First Edition, March 2009

Copyright © 2009 by THE JAMES MADISON CENTER

ISBN-10-0615230717
ISBN-13-9780615230719

Published by
THE JAMES MADISON CENTER
MSC 7402 Johnston Hall Room 222
800 South Main Street
Harrisonburg, VA 22807
http://www.jmu.edu/madison/center/

Revolutions without blood, government without nobles or kings;
To all nations who are not yet free—the examples of the
American Revolution and Constitution.

A TOAST OFFERED ON
JULY 4, 1798

With gratitude to the

ROLLER-BOTTIMORE
FOUNDATION

Contents

Acknowledgments

Liberty and Learning was first conceived during a planning meeting with Janet Wendelken from JMU's Office of Development. During that time, we discussed the need for a concise book on James Madison, which would help make this most enigmatic of founders more accessible and relevant to our university's student body as well as to K-12 students from around the country. Janet quickly became the book's greatest advocate, and she successfully elicited the assistance of the Roller-Bottimore Foundation in Richmond for the project. Through its financial generosity and commitment to public education, *Liberty and Learning* has become a reality. We are grateful for their confidence and support.

We are indebted to the many Madison scholars and researchers who have compiled volumes of his original correspondence and official documents. David Mattern's work as editor of the Madison papers at the University of Virginia is truly extraordinary and indispensable. Likewise, Holly Shulman and Catherine Algor have provided similar exceptional scholarship on the life of Dolley Madison. The three-volume set of Jefferson and Madison's correspondence, *The Republic of Letters*, compiled by James Morton Smith has been particularly helpful in chronicling the friendship between these two extraordinary men. There are several excellent biographies of Madison that we have routinely consulted as well, including Irving Brant's *The Fourth President: A Life of James Madison*, Drew McCoy's *The Last of the Fathers: James Madison & the Republican Legacy*, and Ralph Ketchum's seminal *James Madison: A Biography*.

In our quest to learn more about James Madison's first teacher, Donald Robertson, we visited the King and Queen County Historical Society and were granted complete access to their historical records and files. We were also given the opportunity to visit the site of Robertson's remarkable school, although, sadly, nothing of it remains today. At the Virginia Historical Society, we were able to view Robertson's original journal, which partially chronicles the early studies of the young Madison. They are fascinating records, and some of these pages are printed here for the first time. The James Madison Center maintains an annual scholarship for a pre-service elementary teacher named in Donald Robertson's honor. Madison once said of Robertson, "All that I have been in my life I owe largely to that man," a wonderful testament to the impact that great teachers can have on their students' lives. We have awarded five scholarships by the time of this printing. The recipients are Kimberly Burdette (2005), Melody Mersiovski (2006), Jessica Arms (2007), Shannon Thatcher (2008), and Michelle Ritner (2008). All financial proceeds that result from subsequent sales of *Liberty and Learning* will be used to sustain and endow this important scholarship.

Since its inception in 2005, the 1787 Society has provided support and guidance to the James Madison Center. Several of its members have been particularly helpful in the publication and distribution of this book, including Tommy Bluestein, Caitlin Tracy, Hillary Back, Bethany Riley, Michelle Pillor, Alyssa Johnson, John Sutter, Elizabeth Faust-Shucker, Chelsea Whitley, Casey Boutwell, and Lawrence Lewis. Dan Horton and Hillary Back, two of the students from our History 316 class, "The Life and Times of James Madison 1751-1836," provided additional research on Madison and slavery and on the restoration of Montpelier.

At Montpelier, James Madison's home in Orange County, we would like to acknowledge the help and guidance provided by the staff, particularly the expertise of Beth Taylor, the director of education. We also had the wonderful opportunity to discuss Dolley Madison's son with Ann Miller, who has done an enormous amount of research on the elusive and habitually intoxicated Payne Todd. We had the opportunity to visit his grave at Congressional Cemetery in Washington, D.C., thanks to Joyce Palmer, the chairman of education and outreach. She also allowed us to view and photograph the original interment records for both Payne and Dolley (whose remains were held in the Public and Causten vaults for eight years after her death in 1849). Matt Fulgham, the Assistant Director of Legislative Affairs at the National Archives, was extremely helpful in providing access to many Madison-era primary sources.

Dr. Dorothy Boyd-Rush, professor of history at JMU, has been extremely helpful in conducting research and in assisting with the indexing of this work. We are also particularly appreciative for the fine work done by Shay Cochrane, public relations specialist for the James Madison Center. She is a professional photographer, she has done yeoman's work in compiling, editing, and archiving the photos and illustrations for *Liberty and Learning*. She has also been indispensable in the editing and production of this book. Mishay Whitsitt, graduate assistant for the James Madison Center, has likewise been extremely helpful throughout this entire process.

We have been fortunate to work with many outstanding professionals, including writer Martha Graham, Pam Brock, who has served as the book's editor, and

Bill Thompson, who has done the layout and graphic design. At R.R. Donnelley, we would like to thank both Kaye Sutterer and Steve Herring for advice, direction, and expertise.

We would also like to acknowledge with gratitude Dr. Lee Congdon, JMU professor emeritus of history. Lee is a true scholar and academic; his wisdom, insight, and example remain inspirational. He has made an impact on the lives of countless students while teaching at JMU and continues to advance truth and learning through his research and writing.

Finally, we would be remiss in not acknowledging the exemplary leadership of Dr. Linwood H. Rose, president of James Madison University. Dr. Rose has elevated James Madison's legacy through his strong commitment to public education, teacher training, and civic engagement. At James Madison University, Mr. Madison's legacy is alive and well.

— Philip Bigler and Annie Lorsbach

James Madison, the Man

1723 Ambrose Madison, the grandfather of the future president, and his brother-in-law, Thomas Chew, are deeded 4,675 acres of Piedmont land—the site of the construction of the Montpelier estate.

1732 Ambrose Madison dies, allegedly from poisoning by slaves.

1735 Orange County, Virginia, is created from the western part of Spotsylvania County.

1749 James Madison Sr. marries Nelly Conway.

1751 James Madison Jr. is born on March 16 at Port Conway, Virginia.

1753 Donald Robertson arrives in Virginia.

1758 Donald Robertson opens his school in King and Queen County, Virginia.

1762 Madison, known as Jemmy, begins attending classes at Donald Robertson's school.

1767 Madison returns to Orange County to study under the Reverend Thomas Martin.

1769 Madison begins classes at the College of New Jersey (now Princeton University) and finishes its four-year program in two years.

1771 Madison graduates from the College of New Jersey.

1772 Madison returns to Montpelier after completing his college studies.

1774 Madison is elected to the Orange County Committee of Safety.

1773 Boston Tea Party

1776 Madison serves on the committee with George Mason to draft the Virginia Declaration of Rights.

1777 The Right Reverend James Madison, Madison's cousin, becomes president of the College of William and Mary.

1780 Madison arrives in Philadelphia as a delegate to the Confederation Congress.

1783 Donald Robertson dies.

1785 Madison, while a member of the Virginia House of Delegates, blocks all efforts to establish state support for churches, culminating in ratification of the Statute for Establishing Religious Freedom.

1787 Madison's draft of the Virginia Plan and his revolutionary three-branch federal system becomes the basis of the American Constitution.

1813   Payne Todd, the son of Dolley Madison, is sent to Europe as part of a peace commission.

1814   Washington is evacuated.

1814   White House is burned by the British on August 24.

1814   Madison vetoes the National Bank Law.

1814   The Treaty of Ghent is signed in December and ends the War of 1812.

1815   Andrew Jackson defeats British forces at New Orleans in January, fifteen days after the treaty is signed, but before word of the treaty reaches New Orleans.

1816   Second Bank of the United States is established, and William Jones is appointed as its president.

1816   The American Colonization Society is formed.

1817   Madison vetoes the bill that would provide federal funding of roads and canals, declaring it unconstitutional.

1817   Madison retires to Montpelier.

1817   Madison is elected president of the Agricultural Society of Albemarle County.

1826   Madison is elected rector of the University of Virginia after Thomas Jefferson's death.

1829   Madison serves as delegate to the Virginia Constitutional Convention in Richmond.

1829   Nelly Conway Madison dies at the age of ninety-seven years.

1831   The Virginia Historical Society is founded, and James Madison is elected an honorary member at the first meeting.

1833   Madison is named president of the American Colonization Society.

1834   Madison writes *Advice for My Country.*

1834   Madison resigns as rector of the University of Virginia.

1836   Madison dies at Montpelier on June 28.

1837   Congress purchases James Madison's notes on the Constitution for $35,000.

1837   Dolley Madison moves to Washington, where she lives with her niece, Anna Payne.

1839   Dolley Madison returns to Montpelier.

1841   Dolley Madison returns to Washington.

1844   Dolley Madison is given an honorary seat on the floor of the House of Representatives.

1844   Dolley Madison sells Montpelier.

1848   Congress authorizes the purchase of James Madison's papers for $25,000.

1849 Dolley Madison dies in Washington on July 12.

1849 Dolley Madison is buried in a public vault at Congressional Cemetery.

1852 Payne Todd dies and is interred at Congressional Cemetery on January 18.

1852 Dolley Madison's remains are moved to the Causten Vault.

1858 Dolley Madison's body is removed from Congressional Cemetery to be buried at Montpelier beside her husband.

James Madison, the Legacy

1938 The State Teacher's College at Harrisonburg, Virginia, is renamed Madison College.

1977 Madison College becomes James Madison University.

1983 Marion Scott Dupont, the last private owner of the original Madison estate, bequeaths Montpelier to the National Trust for Historic Preservation.

1999 JMU creates the James Madison Center.

2001 Efforts around the nation observe the two hundred fiftieth anniversary of James Madison's birth.

2004 Congress officially recognizes September 17 as Constitution Day, and all public educational institutions are required by law to conduct lessons or activities for students to commemorate the day.

2008 The restored Montpelier reopens to the public on Constitution Day with a gala celebration featuring remarks by Chief Justice John Roberts.

2009 The two hundredth anniversary of James Madison's inauguration as the nation's fourth president is recognized.

Foreword

On March 16, 1951, Madison College, as we were then known, held celebrations in honor of James Madison's two hundredth birthday. The day was clear, cool, and breezy as spring approached the bucolic Shenandoah Valley. Dignitaries traveling to attend the celebration included Virginia Governor John S. Battle, U. S. Senator Harry F. Byrd and Congressman Burr Harrison.

The day might have been filled with the scholarly remarks typical of such academic functions held on a small American college campus if it were not for the keynote speech delivered in Wilson Hall Auditorium by Dr. Raymond Pinchbeck, dean of the University of Richmond. So impressed by the speech was Representative Harrison that he returned to Washington, D. C., and redelivered the entire address on the floor of the U. S. House of Representatives so that Pinchbeck's words would perpetually reside in the *Congressional Record*.

As president of James Madison University, I find it especially important that in his remarks Dean Pinchbeck observed the very real link between James Madison, the man, and the institution that bears his name. I quote Dean Pinchbeck's words from that March 21, 1951, edition of the *Congressional Record* in this forward. Pinchbeck said,

> *Two hundred years ago today, James Madison, the Father of the Constitution of the United States, was born. It is fitting that we assemble here, at Madison College, which bears his name, to pay tribute to this great citizen. It was a highly significant and appropriate honor paid James Madison in 1938 when his beloved native Commonwealth of Virginia gave his name to this college, which is dedicated primarily to the preparation of teachers of the youth of Virginia. Madison believed that popular government, political democracy, and human freedom would not long endure without an intelligent and educated citizenry.*

Yet, in a broader context, Pinchbeck made what may have been his most insightful observation about Madison's legacy.

> *Memorials to James Madison have not taken the form of equestrian statues or monuments. The life and services of this gentle and scholarly man must be sought in the libraries of the United States and the free nations of the world.*

This is a subtle yet powerful point. While it is an elegant notion that a memorial to James Madison exists in the libraries of all free nations, historians often wonder why Madison's legacy is not given the same popular attention as other founders, such as Washington, Jefferson, and Adams. As Father of the U. S. Constitution, Madison's accomplishments perhaps are the most important to the perpetuity of our democratic republic.

In this excellent introduction to James Madison, Philip Bigler examines the life of our most brilliant founder and reveals why Madison is worthy of your consideration. Mr. Bigler directs the Madison Center at James Madison University, where he works tirelessly to demonstrate to students of every age how James Madison continues to influence our nation to this very day. While teaching humanities and history at Thomas Jefferson High School for Science and Technology, Mr. Bigler earned the 1998 National Teacher of the Year. I can think of no one better suited to write such a work as this. Throughout his life as a historian, Philip Bigler has been devoted to ensuring that the legacy of our nation's founding fathers lives on in the minds of our youth.

In remarking on that continuing educational imperative, Burr Harrison gave no better reason why Madison matters than in his introduction to Pinchbeck's speech on the House floor.

> *"In the ceremonies at Madison College, the words, the writings of Madison were recalled. As my thoughts were directed once more to the first years of this Republic, I wished that it had been possible for all of the Members of this House to be present. The demands of these crucial days often prevent our contemplation of the basic ideas of our Government and our free society at times in which such consideration would be most beneficial. There, as the principles which Madison expounded and sought to enshrine for his posterity were recalled, I found a reenforcement of the national faith."*

DR. LINWOOD H. ROSE
President
James Madison University

Liberty&Learning

Preface

I n recent years, America's founding fathers have enjoyed a remarkable resurgence in popularity. Even the popular news media have rediscovered these visionary creators of the early republic. *Time* magazine, *U.S. News & World Report*, and other popular periodicals regularly feature cover stories chronicling the legacies of Thomas Jefferson, Benjamin Franklin, and George Washington.[1] To the general public, this secular trinity comprises an American pantheon of wise, unselfish, and civic-minded leaders. Their conduct and achievement serve as an effective counterpoint to the pedestrian debates and petty distractions that too often characterize contemporary political life.

Today's historians are writing prolifically about this founding trio's contributions to the American experiment. Joseph Ellis, in particular, has written several excellent books on the era, including *His Excellency: George Washington, Founding Brothers: The Revolutionary Generation, American Sphinx: The Character of Thomas Jefferson,* and *American Creation: Triumphs and Tragedies at the Founding of the Republic*. Likewise, Bill Brands' widely respected book, *The First American: The Life and Times of Benjamin Franklin*, was a finalist for the Pulitzer Prize and was made into a highly acclaimed PBS special. Other, less-appreciated leaders of the Federalist era have also drawn renewed attention from modern biographers. In 2001, for instance, renowned historian David McCullough received widespread acclaim for his massive, 768-page book, *John Adams*. "David McCullough's new full-scale biography of Adams, a lucid and compelling work that should do for Adams's reputation what Mr. McCullough's 1992 book, *Truman*, did for Harry S Truman,"[2] lauded the *New York Times*. The work did much to restore Adams's historical reputation, which had been severely tarnished by the passage of the notorious Alien and Sedition Acts during his administration as well as by his well-known obstinate and inflexible personality. Adams himself wrote openly about his tainted legacy in 1802. "Having been the Object of Misrepresentation, some of my Posterity may probably wish to see in my own hand

Writing a proof of the falsehood of the Mass of odious Abuse of my Character, with which News Papers, private Letters and public Pamphlets and Histories have been disgraced for thirty Years."[3] For those unwilling to tackle the challenge of the written word, McCullough's lengthy work was transformed by Home Box Office into an easily manageable mini-series featuring the acclaimed actor, Paul Giamatti. The founders, it seems, have become prime-time fare.

A renaissance in nonfiction literature about the origins of America should not be altogether unexpected in times of political and social turmoil.[4] After the September 11 attacks against the United States, the nation's citizenry naturally sought a reaffirmation of the nation's long-held republican principles. The founders, they discovered, still provided timeless wisdom and showed a remarkable perseverance during their own equally difficult times. Through a careful study and understanding of their lives, it is possible to confront modern realities with renewed courage and a sense of conviction.

One of our nation's greatest leaders, though, has remained conspicuously absent from the best-seller lists and from popular history. James Madison remains in the shadows of the past, unjustly portrayed as a mere acolyte to the great Thomas Jefferson. In a letter to Benjamin Rush in 1790, Jefferson himself remarked on this absurdity. Jefferson described Madison as "the greatest man in the world."[5] Their friendship, which spanned six decades, was one of equals.

It is perplexing that Madison appears to have been forgotten, while so many of his contemporaries have been resurrected from obscurity. Even a recent, albeit modest, 164-page biography about Madison failed to do this great patriot justice or provide him with suitable respect. Published as part of a larger series on American Presidents, the book inexplicably featured a full-page picture of James Monroe (instead of Madison) opposite its title page.[6]

In today's celebrity culture, charisma and fame have become confused for substance and significance. James Madison would not have fared well in such a media-driven culture. His writings were scholarly, his arguments nuanced, and his allegories classical. Worse, he was short in physical stature and unassuming in public venues. Yet Madison remains a true visionary who keenly understood human nature, complete with all of its flaws and foibles. He fully realized the dangers inherent in the concentration of power, in the potential of tyrannies of the majority, and in the lust for popularity. Thus it was James Madison who carefully orchestrated the design for a government that would provide stability for society, control the unrestrained passions of its people, and maximize human liberty. We hope this book provides a better understanding of the man who was rightfully known as the Father of the United States Constitution.

ENDNOTES

[1] See "The Radical Mind of Thomas Jefferson," *Time*, July 5, 2004, and "The Amazing Adventures of Benjamin Franklin," *Time*, July 7, 2003. *U.S. News & World Report* also did a cover story in 2001 on Joseph Ellis' book, *Founding Brothers*.

[2] Machiko Kakutani, "Rediscovering John Adams, the Founder Time Forgot," Books of the Times, *New York Times*, May 22, 2001. http://www.nytimes.com (Accessed July 23, 2008)

[3] James Bishop Peabody, ed., *John Adams, A Biography in His Own Words* (New York: Newsweek, 1977), 18.

[4] The use of the word "literature" is intentional since historians are now writing in narrative and engaging prose.

[5] James Morton Smith, ed., *The Republic of Letters: the Correspondence between Thomas Jefferson and James Madison 1776-1826* (New York: W.W. Norton & Company, 1995), 648.

[6] Monroe and Madison bore no resemblance to each other. Monroe was six feet tall and seven years younger than the five-feet-four James Madison. Apparently the book's publishers were made aware of this egregious error and quickly rushed into print a replacement edition. Another glaring error that was corrected by republication was the assertion that the Constitutional Convention (1787) was portrayed in "the delightful musical *1776*."

CHAPTER ONE

Monuments, Memorials, and Madison

*I've decided that the best dreamer was Madison ... I think I know ...
what Madison's dream was. It was a dream of a new land to fulfill with
people in self-control."* — ROBERT FROST

A nation's values can easily be discerned by a careful study of what its citizens and leaders choose to memorialize. These bronze and marble monuments accurately reflect a sense of common history, and, more importantly, they reveal what individuals, events, ideals, and beliefs a society cherishes. For the United States, the capital of Washington, D.C., has become a virtual microcosm of the country's history and the center of our national identity. Citizens and tourists alike regularly make the pilgrimage to this grand city in an effort to gain a better understanding of what being an American truly means.

During the American Revolution and even after the subsequent ratification of the United States Constitution, the seat of government moved with surprising regularity.[1] Ultimately, Congress decided that no existing colonial-era city was sufficiently adequate to permanently house the newly formed government. To architecturally reflect the founders' grand vision for a new American republic, an entirely new federal city would have to be constructed, and it would rise like a mythical phoenix from a virtual wilderness. After much debate, deliberation, and compromise, Congress selected a site along the banks of the Potomac

River for the creation of a ten-mile, square federal district that would be completely independent of influence and interference from the states. Construction began in 1792 on the capital's major buildings, but the government was unable to occupy them until the fall of 1800. Then, dozens of wagons and carts loaded with important files, papers, documents, and furniture made the arduous trek from Philadelphia. Soon the entire government, comprising a staff of just 136 employees, followed. The U.S. Congress formally convened on November 17 in the modest, uncompleted north wing of the new Capitol building, which was strategically located on the top of Jenkins's Hill, the precise geographic center of the District of Columbia. John Adams (now a lame-duck president, having been recently defeated by Thomas Jefferson in the hotly contested election of 1800) became the first inhabitant of the specially constructed executive mansion. His wife, Abigail, was suitably unimpressed with her new surroundings, astutely observing, "Our location is far from being pleasant or even convenient. Around the Capitol are seven or eight boarding houses, one tailor, one shoemaker, one printer, a washing-woman, a grocery shop, a pamphlet and stationery shop, a small dry goods shop, and an oyster house. This makes the whole of the Federal City as connected with the Capitol."[2]

It took several decades before Washington evolved into a metropolis worthy of a great country. The city's distinctive classical-revival architecture slowly began to replace the rows of run-down boardinghouses, repulsive taverns, and ugly tenements that had defined the early city. These gleaming white marble temples of the American republic were not only functional, but they served as a perpetual architectural reminder of the founders' civic inspiration from ancient Greece and Rome.

In 1833, a private citizens group undertook plans to construct the city's first important memorial. The Washington Monument would appropriately honor the American Revolution's greatest hero and the republic's first president. Actual construction began fifteen years later, yet ceased soon thereafter due to a growing north-south sectionalism, which ultimately led to the onset of the Civil War. Forty years elapsed before the 555-foot obelisk was completed; today it remains the most visible feature of the capital's skyline.

Over the ensuing years, the nation would honor other great American presidents with their own monuments in Washington. Anchoring the far west end of the national mall is the Lincoln Memorial. It is a true American Parthenon complete with its thirty-six impressive Doric columns (one for each state of the

PHILIP BIGLER

union in 1861) and gargantuan statue of the Great Emancipator, Abraham Lincoln. Nearby is the Jefferson Memorial. Built during the darkest days of World War II to remind Americans of the country's founding principles, it is reminiscent of both the Pantheon in Rome and the Rotunda at the University of Virginia. The Jefferson Memorial is nestled among the city's renowned cherry trees and pays appropriate tribute to the author of the Declaration of Independence.[3] The most recent presidential monument was dedicated in 1997 and is devoted to Franklin Delano Roosevelt. Even "lesser presidents" such as Andrew Jackson and Ulysses S. Grant have their own monuments in Washington, although their statues are in recognition for their military service rather than their political careers.

A view of the nation's capital from Arlington Heights. The design and architecture of Washington, D.C., reflect James Madison's philosophical beliefs for the establishment of a new republic based upon the principles outlined in the U.S. Constitution.

Throughout Washington, D.C., there are countless other statues strategically positioned at traffic circles and key intersections. They honor many of the nation's once-prominent military heroes, including William Tecumseh Sherman, David Farragut, Nathaniel Green, Winfield Scott Hancock, and Thomas Logan. Even the great physicist and naturalized American citizen, Albert Einstein, is remembered with a modernesque statue in front of the National Academy for the Sciences. Curiously, near the Jefferson Memorial is an isolated statue of the Virginia statesman, George Mason. A notorious curmudgeon and author of the Virginia Declaration of Rights, Mason committed an act of historical suicide by refusing to sign the U.S. Constitution, and today few tourists recognize this once well-known figure.

Surprisingly absent from this huge and impressive display of commemorative history is any real monument to James Madison, the Father of the United States Constitution. This is odd, given that, during his lifetime, Madison was widely recognized for his contributions in the creation of the American republic. Indeed, many towns across the nation still bear his name although few of today's inhabitants are aware of their origins. Yet in Washington, D.C., there are no Madison memorials, nor are there any substantive statues or patriotic displays for this most important founding father. True, one of the buildings at the Library of Congress has been named in James Madison's honor, but it is a contemporary, undistinguished structure—a place of solitude and contemplation reserved for scholars and researchers—rarely on the itinerary of tourists to the city. The thousands of casual visitors to the library far prefer to visit the adjacent Jefferson Building to see its impressive Italian marble, highly decorated vaulted ceilings, and inspiring main reading room. So, it seems that in memorial architecture, James Madison's legacy has been forgotten, and he is overshadowed even in death by his good friend, Thomas Jefferson.

To the astute observer, though, Madison's presence can be found everywhere throughout Washington in ways that are not traditional or overt, but as clever as the man himself. The very layout and design of the federal city reflects Madison's clear vision for an American government, created by the people, and with clearly delineated powers that would maximize human liberty and ensure its citizens the fundamental right to pursue happiness in the manner of their own choosing. Washington's grand boulevards were consciously designed to accentuate the independent and symbolic relationship between the various branches of government (the legislative, executive, and judiciary) along with Madison's firm belief in the separation of powers and in the checks and balances that were codified in the U.S. Constitution. Appropriately, the city's main thoroughfare is named Constitution Avenue (flanked by Independence and Pennsylvania Avenues). The National Archives is probably one of its best-known features.[4] Here is the nation's repository for its most momentous documents. Its staff of historians, preservationists, and archivists serves as the caretaker of the country's history. Enshrined in the rotunda of the building, protected by bulletproof glass and encased in argon gas, are the three documents central to American history—the Declaration of Independence, the U.S. Constitution, and the Bill of Rights—collectively known as the American creed.[5] James Madison was the instrumental force behind the writing of two of these landmark documents. For him, being an American was not a geographic distinction, a religious affiliation or an ethnic identity. It was rather an essential belief in the philosophy defined by these documents. Madison, more than all of his contemporaries, demonstrated the power of ideas by constructing an enduring form of government from them. His belief in a free republic never wavered, despite intense political divisions and sectional strife. Madison's vision for America has proven far more powerful and valuable than anything man has yet formulated out of stone or marble.[6] To find Madison's monument, one needs merely to look to the American constitutional government, which has endured for more than two centuries. It is James Madison's gift to the world.

The Rotunda of the National Archives in Washington, D.C. On permanent display are the three founding documents of the American republic: The Declaration of Independence, the Constitution, and the Bill of Rights.

ENDNOTES

Epigraph: Robert Frost quoted in James Morton Smith, 1.

[1]Due to military necessities during the Revolution, Congress met in various cities, including Lancaster, Trenton, Princeton, York, Annapolis, and Philadelphia. During most of the Confederation period, the capital of the United States was New York City. The Constitution in Article I, Section 8, grants Congress the power to legislate "over such District (not exceeding ten Miles square) as may, by Cession of particular States, and the Acceptance of Congress, become the Seat of the Government of the United States." James Madison was instrumental in negotiating the move of the capital to the south. This story is thoroughly explained in Joseph Ellis' book, *Founding Brothers*, in the chapter titled "The Dinner," 48-80.

[2]Abigail Adams quoted in Philip Bigler, *Washington in Focus: A Photo History of the Nation's Capital* (St. Petersburg: Vandamere Press, 1994), 14.

[3]Memorials often represent our preferred view of history rather than an accurate reporting of the facts. Christopher Hitchens notes in his book, *Thomas Jefferson: Author of America*, that one of the inscriptions on the Jefferson Memorial is fundamentally misleading. The passage inscribed in stone reads: "Nothing is more certainly written in the book of fate, than that these people are to be free ..." It implies Jefferson's strong and enlightened opposition to slavery, but, Hitchens explains, "Only the first eighteen words of this passage are incised in stone on the Jefferson Memorial ... [done so] ... in a moment of optimism about human rights, on Jefferson's bicentennial in April 1943." The omitted portion of the continuing passage, however, is much darker. Jefferson continues: "... nor is it less certain that the two races, equally free, cannot live in the same government. Nature, habit, opinion have drawn indelible lines of distinction between them." See Christopher Hitchens, *Thomas Jefferson: Author of America* (New York: HarperCollins, 2005), 34.

[4]Some believe that the naming of Pennsylvania Avenue, the road that prominently connects the White House with the Capitol, was intended to pacify the citizens of that state for the loss of the capital, which was relocated from Philadelphia to the District in 1800.

[5]In 2004, the film *National Treasure* starring Nicholas Cage, brought the National Archives briefly into the mainstream of American popular culture. Although it sparked popular interest in the Archives, the film was little more than an American version of the *DaVinci Code*. Its portrayal of the theft of the Declaration of Independence is sheer fantasy. There are no secret clues or hidden messages contained in the Declaration. On the back of the document is merely the inscription: "Original Declaration of Independence / dated 4th July 1776." Interestingly, though, since the document is now backlit for the first time, a mysterious handprint on the document of unknown origins is visible for the first time.

[6]This is true with the notable exception of Thomas Jefferson, whose ideas in the Declaration of Independence remain fundamental to the United States and to the world. Jefferson wished to be remembered for three things on his tombstone—"Author of the Declaration of Independence, Of the Statute of Virginia for Religious Freedom; and Father of the University of Virginia." Jefferson's epitaph along with a brief biography is available at: http://www.monticello.org/jefferson/biography.html.

CHAPTER TWO

Piedmont, Princeton, and an Educated Citizenry

*The calm and philosophic temper of Mr. Madison, the purity of his character,
the sincerity of his patriotism, and the sagacity of his intellect {inspired}
universal trust.* — JOHN PENDLETON KENNEDY

I n the twenty-fourth year of the reign of His Majesty, George II of England, the British Empire was rapidly expanding, and its colonial possessions had made it prosperous. Only the French and Louis XV posed any serious rival to England's global supremacy. The British sugar islands in the tropical Caribbean had proven to be a continuous source of wealth, while the king's coffers were regularly replenished by tobacco revenues from Virginia and by an occasional state-sponsored piracy. King George's loyal subjects throughout the colonies considered themselves fortunate to be citizens of the freest and most enlightened empire on earth. It was into this world that James Madison Jr. was born on March 16, 1751.[1]

Virginians had always considered themselves to be the most British of all of the colonies, and they were fiercely defensive of their heritage. Most counties in Virginia derived their names from British nobility, including Albemarle, Botetourt, Caroline, Fairfax, Hanover, King George, Queen Anne, Prince William, and Westmoreland.

The colony had been established at Jamestown in May 1607 and earned its epithet, the Old Dominion, because of its support of the British crown during the darkest days of the English civil war and the nightmare that was Oliver Cromwell.

The first settlers to the Virginia colony were clustered along the banks of the James River within easy access to the Chesapeake Bay and the Atlantic Ocean. They were almost wholly dependent upon a steady supply of food and staples from Britain along with an ample quantity of replacement settlers who were needed to fill the void left by those who seemed to die so easily in the New World. In fact, Jamestown's early years were punctuated by famine, pestilence, and plague. Virginia regularly and repeatedly teetered toward financial failure and catastrophic collapse until it finally achieved economic salvation through the introduction of tobacco in 1612 by John Rolfe. The Stuart King, James I, was initially unenthusiastic and hated the new fad of smoking, describing it as

> *a custome loathsome to the eye, hatefull to the nose, harmefull to the braine, dangerous to the lungs and in the blacke stinking fume thereof, nearest resembling the horrible Stigian smoke of the pit that is bottomless.*[2]

His opposition to tobacco, though, was quickly mitigated by the steady stream of revenue generated from his subjects' insatiable demand for the noxious crop.

As the global demand for tobacco increased with improved supply, British mercantile policy soon required that all shipments from the colonies be sent first to England before being marketed and sold to other nations. In Virginia, land and labor were both in great demand as thousands of new arrivals flocked to America to seek their fortunes. The colony's most successful and wealthy settlers were those who had arrived early in the seventeenth century and had established their plantations along the banks of the colony's tidal waters with the closest and quickest access to British ports.[3] These individuals became known as the First Families of Virginia (FFVs) and included the Burwells, Byrds, Carters, and Randolphs.

The quest for cultivable lands led later arriving generations of Virginia settlers to move inland to the gently rolling hills of the piedmont, far beyond the fall lines of the colony's great rivers.[4] In 1732, Ambrose Madison, his wife, Frances Taylor, and their three children relocated from Caroline County to a remote and primitive plantation known as Mount Pleasant in what would later become Orange County. The fertile tobacco fields were farmed by a considerable number of slaves, and the small manor house on the property was undistinguished but had a remarkable view of the Blue Ridge Mountains.[5]

The cultivation, harvesting, and curing of tobacco required an enormous amount of physical labor. The importation of slaves was instigated to meet this demand, and, by 1660, slavery had become firmly entrenched in Virginia and

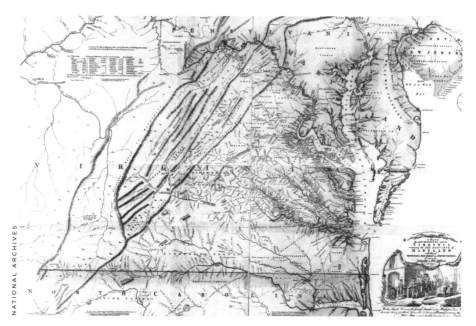

NATIONAL ARCHIVES

The Fry-Jefferson Map of Virginia, 1751. Virginia had four distinct geographical zones—tidewater, the piedmont, the valley, and the mountain west. The most desirable tobacco plantations were located on the navigable rivers of the tidewater because they had quick access to the Atlantic Ocean.

her sister colonies. What relationship Ambrose Madison had with his slaves is unknowable, but shortly after his arrival at the Mount Pleasant estate, he fell seriously ill, apparently poisoned. Madison died on August 27, 1732, and three slaves were arrested "for feloniously Conspiring the Death of Ambrose Madison."[6] Ultimately, one was hanged, and the other two received twenty-nine lashes each.[7]

At 32 years old, Ambrose's widow, Frances, was left to manage the frontier plantation on her own and never remarried. Her eldest son, James Madison (the father

PHILIP BIGLER

The historical road marker along U.S. 301 that indicates the birthplace of James Madison. Madison was born at his mother's ancestral home at Port Conway, Virginia, on March 16, 1751.

of the president), gradually assumed greater responsibilities for running the estate as he grew into maturity. He frequently traveled to Port Royal and Port Conway, two tobacco ports on opposite shores of the Rappahannock River, to conduct business.[8]

A depiction of the original Mount Pleasant homestead. Ambrose Madison, the president's grandfather, settled in the Virginia piedmont in 1732. Within just a few months, he allegedly was fatally poisoned by his slaves. The president's father built a more suitable mansion in the 1760s, and the Mount Pleasant site fell into disrepair. Today, archaeology students from James Madison University have been involved in efforts to rediscover the site's earliest remnants.

There he gained the acquaintance of Eleanor "Nelly" Conway, and the couple married in 1749. They made their home at Mount Pleasant, which by now Madison owned outright in accordance with the terms of his father's original will.

Perhaps because of Mount Pleasant's isolation, Nelly chose to travel more than fifty miles to her mother's home in Port Conway to give birth to her first child. There on March 16, 1751 (NS), according to the family Bible, James Madison Jr. was born.

> *James Madison junr. Was born on Tuesday Night at 12 o'Clock it being the last of the 5ᵗʰ. & beginning of the 6ᵗʰ. Day of March 1750-1 for god-Fathers Mr. John Moore & Mr. Jonathn. Gibson & for God-Mothers Mrs. Rebecca Moore, Miss Judith Catless and Miss Elizabeth Catlett.*[9]

The Madison family expanded rapidly. Over the ensuing decade, six of eleven more children joined James and Nelly's firstborn, who came to be known in the family as Jemmy.[10] The original Mount Pleasant farmhouse quickly became too small and crowded for such a large family, so, between 1763 and 1765, the senior Madison supervised the construction of a more substantive and appropriate home. Located just a short distance away from the original homestead, the two-story brick mansion became known as Montpelier and was considered to be one of the most impressive homes in the entire piedmont region of Virginia.[11]

As a child, little Jemmy received a rudimentary education from his mother and grandmother. In 1762, at the age of eleven, he left home to board with Donald Robertson, a renowned educator who had established a small school on his modest farm in King and Queen County. It proved to be a fortuitous decision, because Madison excelled under Robertson's tutelage. He would later remember his first teacher as "a man of extensive learning, and a distinguished teacher."[12]

A page from Donald Robertson's journal listing some of the books used for instruction at his boarding school in King and Queen County. Included in the inventory are such works as Milton's *Paradise Lost,* Plutarch's *Lives*, and Aesop's *Fables,* as well as the Greek classical histories of Thucydides and Herodotus. Robertson was Madison's teacher for five years. He would later say of Robertson, "All I have been in life I largely owe to that man."

Donald Robertson had arrived in Virginia in March 1753 and, for the next five years, served as a tutor on a plantation of John Baylor in Caroline County. He eventually settled in Drysdale Parish on a 150-acre estate along the banks of the Mattaponi River.[13] By the time he opened his school, Robertson had acquired an extensive library that consisted of more than sixty volumes, which he freely circulated among his students.[14] For the young James Madison, Robertson's school provided an opportunity to read and explore books that had been unavailable to him on the Virginia frontier. As historian Douglass Adair notes, "Here, in the Scotch classicist's [Robertson's] library, the first of any scope to which young Madison had access, he began to discover for himself the resources hidden in books."[15]

It was also at Robertson's school that Madison was seriously exposed to the exciting and radical ideas of the Scottish Enlightenment. He studied some of the era's greatest political philosophers, including Montesquieu and Locke. In addition, he read Horace, Virgil, Plato, Thucydides, Tacitus, Milton, and Justinian while studying a variety of subjects, including French, Greek, Latin, Algebra, grammar, composition, history, geometry, and literature.[16] These early years away from home helped Madison discover for himself a love of learning, and he began to develop the skills that would make him a lifelong scholar. Historian David Mays claims, "The quality of Robertson's instruction was so high that his pupils were to have enormous influence in shaping the history of Virginia and the United States."[17] Well after Madison had retired, he had the occasion to reflect upon his long career and readily acknowledged, "All that I have been in my life, I owe largely to this man."[18]

When Madison returned to the Montpelier plantation in 1767, he met Thomas Martin, the new pastor of the Brick Church in Orange. In addition to his clerical duties, Martin had been engaged by the senior Madison to serve as a tutor for his children as well as to assist James in preparing for college admittance. Martin was a recent graduate of the College of New Jersey, and he urged Madison to consider attending classes there despite the fact that very few Southerners ever ventured north for schooling. Virtually all sons of the Virginia gentry who even attempted higher education preferred the more predictable and comfortable confines of the College of William and Mary in Williamsburg.[19]

William and Mary was hardly known for its high academic standards. Many viewed it as a finishing school for the Virginia elite, a place to have a brief respite before returning to plantation society and life as a tobacco farmer.[20] The students and faculty of the college were widely known to enjoy horse racing, gaming, cockfighting, and other frivolities and were frequent patrons of the many taverns located along Duke of Gloucester Street in Williamsburg. Philip Fithian, a graduate of the College of New Jersey who served briefly as a tutor at Nomini Hall in Westmoreland County, wrote of a discussion he had with his employer, Robert Carter. Fithian said,

. . . We conversed on many things, & at length on the College of William & Mary at Williamsburg. He informed me that it is in such confusion at present, & so badly directed, that he cannot send his Children with propriety there for Improvement & useful Education—That he has known the Professors to play all Night at Cards in publick Houses in the City, and has often seen them drunken in the Street.[21]

For Madison, whose health was often precarious, the prospect of studying in the tidewater region of Virginia could be potentially fatal. The climate, he noted, "was unhealthy for persons going from a mountainous region."[22]

Martin's influence upon Madison's final decision to attend the College of New Jersey was certainly considerable, but further encouragement came from the exciting news that the Reverend John Witherspoon had assumed the presidency of the university in 1768. Witherspoon had already achieved a stellar reputation as an extraordinary teacher and a man of keen intellect. His appointment had the immediate effect of elevating the university's reputation and prestige.

For Madison, his summer 1769 trip north was the first time he had left Virginia. It would prove to be an opportunity for him to break free from the strong provincialism of his home colony. Accompanying Madison on the journey was a Montpelier slave, Sawney, and Thomas Martin, his tutor. The ten-day trek was both difficult and dangerous, requiring the small Madison party to traverse poorly maintained roads and to ford numerous streams and rivers. Upon his arrival in Philadelphia, though, Madison encountered a cosmopolitan city of unimaginable size and wonderment. Here, according to Ralph Ketcham, "Madison saw for the first time such wonders as stone sidewalks and paved streets lighted at night, row on row of three-story brick dwellings, churches of eight different denominations within a few blocks of each other, and many other public buildings, including two libraries, the Pennsylvania Hospital, the Academy of Philadelphia, the State House, and a barracks for nearly two thousand soldiers."[23]

NATIONAL ARCHIVES

The skyline of colonial Philadelphia. Madison first visited this cosmopolitan city in 1769 while en route to study at the College of New Jersey.

After a brief respite there, Madison completed his journey to Princeton. The entire academic portion of the College of New Jersey was confined to a single building, Nassau Hall. Built in 1756 and named for William III (of the House of Orange-Nassau), the three-story structure housed the school's classrooms, the campus library, dining facilities, and student dormitories. It was an intentionally austere environment, one that accorded the students few luxuries, temptations, or diversions. Crowded three to a room, Madison immediately immersed himself with his studies, since he had arrived at mid term and was seriously behind his classmates. A few weeks later, he wrote to the Reverend Thomas Martin.

> *I am perfectly pleased with my present situation; and the prospect before me of three years confinement, however terrible it may sound, has nothing in it, but what will be greatly alleviated by the advantages I hope to derive from it.*[24]

During Madison's matriculation, the College of New Jersey was filled with a youthful zeal and enthusiasm for the ever-growing patriot cause. The student body was collectively angry over the many perceived British provocations that had been most recently exemplified by the imposition of the Townshend Duties and the writs of assistance (which allowed warrantless searches for contraband and smuggled goods). In open protest of British imperial policy, many of the students periodically wore "American clothe" to show their support of non-importation agreements. The young James Madison joined the newly formed Whig Society—a social debating club that professed allegiance to time-honored, sacred British principles that were routinely violated by the current King and Parliament. While at the College, Madison also became friends with William Bradford, Aaron Burr, and Philip Freneau, all of whom were destined to play significant roles in the birth and evolution of the American republic.

By all accounts, Madison was a serious scholar at Princeton. Here he refined the important skills required for serious research and developed the ability to use precise logic and engage in persuasive argument. As Merrill Peterson accurately noted, Princeton prided itself on its ability to "cultivate reason and critical inquiry" in its students.[25]

For Madison, college life was liberating, and he fully embraced the important ideals of the Enlightenment, which emphasized human reason, Newtonian science, and rational thought. Through extensive reading and study, Madison began to develop his own burgeoning political philosophy. It was grounded on the principle that a government's primary role was to provide societal stability while maximizing human liberty and ensuring its citizens their "unalienable" rights to pursue their own personal happiness. Government, Madison believed, was a creation of man and a solemn contract designed to protect liberty and promote social harmony. In an era where monarchies, pashas, tyrannies, and despots still dominated, his beliefs were truly revolutionary.

Through sheer determination and hard work, the young Madison was able to complete his academic studies in just two years, but his rigorous, self-imposed regimen came at the expense of his health. In a letter written in 1773 to Madison, William Bradford commented, "You alarm me, by what you tell me about your health. I believe you hurt your constitution while here, by too close an application to study; but I hope 'tis not so bad with you as you seem to imagine. Persons of the weakest Constitutions by taking a proper care of themselves often out live those of the strongest."[26] Madison was too ill to attend his own commencement exercises in 1771, let alone risk the difficult journey to return home to Virginia. Instead, he spent the following year engaged in post-graduate studies under the direct supervision of the Reverend John Witherspoon, using this time to study Hebrew and theology. The academic life was invigorating for Madison; scholarly pursuits and the world of books had a far greater appeal to him than a life of drudgery managing tobacco production and wasting time in the frivolous leisure pursuits of the carefree Virginia gentry.

When Madison did finally return home to Montpelier in 1772, he once again resided with his parents and their still-expanding family. It would prove to be one of the most emotionally trying periods of Madison's life, filled with youthful angst and mental anguish at the prospect of a future that was all too ordinary and predictable. In truth, Madison was directionless and uncertain about what he hoped to do with his life, readily acknowledging, "My customary enjoyments [are] Solitude and Contemplation."[27] During this time, he helped out around the plantation and assumed the primary responsibil-

The Reverend John Witherspoon. Witherspoon was the newly appointed president of the College of New Jersey at the time of Madison's matriculation. He served as Madison's academic mentor and would later become the only clergyman to sign the Declaration of Independence.

ity for tutoring three of his siblings (William, Sarah, and Elizabeth) "in some of the first rudiments of literature but it does not take up so much of my time."[28] Madison also began to read and explore the law, apparently motivated more out of boredom than by any strong avocation. He was in frequent correspondence with his college friend, William Bradford, and sometimes the two reminisced about their carefree days at Princeton. "The value of a college-life like most other blessing[s] is seldom known but by its loss," wrote Bradford in 1772. "I little thought I should have regretted my leaving Nassau Hall so much as I feel I do ... I leave Nassau Hall with the same regret that a fond son would feel who parts with an indulgent mother to tempt the dangers of the sea."[29]

The onset of the American Revolution, though, offered many ambitious young men unprecedented opportunity. James Madison was soon drawn into the political conflict, personally outraged by the punitive British actions against the Massachusetts colony following the Boston Tea Party. As his home colony quickly became radicalized, Madison was elected to the Orange County Committee of Safety in 1774 and was later promoted to the rank of colonel with the local militia. He proudly boasted about his military unit's abilities as well as his own accuracy with a musket.

> The strength of this Colony will lie chiefly in the rifle-men of the Upland Counties, of whom we shall have great numbers. You would be astonished at the perfection this art is brought to. The most inexpert hands rec[k]on it an indifferent shot to miss the bigness of a man's face at the distance of 100 Yards. I am far from being among the best & should not often miss it on a fair trial at that distance.[30]

Despite such bravado, Madison's military career was confined to occasional musters and drills, since his poor health precluded the true hardships of a regular army life.[31]

In 1776, Madison was elected to serve as the Orange County representative to the revolutionary government then being formed in Williamsburg; thus began what would be lifelong political service to the nation. Madison served on George Mason's committee to draft the Virginia Declaration of Rights, and he quickly earned the reputation of bringing a scholar's sense of inquiry and integrity to virtually every important issue. Allies and opponents alike were impressed with the sophistication and wisdom of Madison's arguments as well as the thoroughness of his preparation. It was obvious to all that his education at the College of New Jersey had served him extremely well.

Over the next several years, as the new American nation struggled, Madison continued to formulate and refine his political beliefs. He concluded that a republic was the best form of government to secure and preserve the liberties of the people. He predicated his logic on historical precedent and tempered his logic with a keen understanding of the realities of human nature. A well informed, educated, and virtuous citizenry was critical to the survival of a nation founded upon such principles. To help ensure this, Madison became an early proponent for advancing learning throughout the states by creating new schools and colleges. "Knowledge will forever govern ignorance: and a people who mean to be their own governours, must arm themselves with the power which knowledge gives,"[32] Madison wrote. His close friend, Thomas Jefferson, concurred. "Enlighten the people generally, and tyranny and oppressions of body and mind will vanish like evil spirits at the dawn of day. . . . I believe it [human condition] susceptible of much improvement . . . and that the diffusion of knowledge among the people is to be the instrument by which it is affected."[33]

In 1796, President George Washington, in his final address to Congress, took the initiative by urging the creation of a new, national university of the United States. Such an institution, he believed, would provide a sense of pride and culture in the United States. Washington elaborated, "The assembly to which I address myself is too enlightened not to be fully sensible how much a flourishing state of the arts and sciences contributes to national prosperity and reputation."[34] Moreover, Washington hoped that this new university would attract the finest professors and teachers and would offer a high-quality education to the nation's best students. It would have the added benefit of increasing a sense of nationalism and unity while advancing knowledge. Washington explained the situation to Congress.

> *Amongst the motives to such an institution, the assimilation of the principles, opinions, and manners of our country-men by the common education of a portion of our youth from every quarter well deserves attention. The more homogenous our citizens can be made in these particulars the greater will be our prospect of permanent union; and a primary object of such a national institution should be the education of our youth in the science of government. In a republic what species of knowledge can be equally important and what duty more pressing on its legislature than to patronize a plan for communicating it to those who are to be the future guardians of the liberties of the country?[35]*

Representative James Madison enthusiastically supported Washington's proposal by sponsoring legislation in the House of Representatives for the "establishment of a university within the District of Columbia."[36] Unfortunately, with the advent of the new Adams administration, growing political divisions, foreign policy concerns, and Madison's own retirement from Congress, his legislation languished and disappeared without becoming law.

It would take another fourteen years before the idea of a national university would again be resurrected. In 1810, President James Madison urged Congress to enact legislation to create a College of the United States despite the ominous and steady approach of war. His arguments for such an institution were eloquent and persuasive.

> *Whilst it is universally admitted that a well-instructed people alone can be permanently a free people, and whilst it is evident that the means of diffusing and improving useful knowledge from so small a proportion of the expenditures for national purposes, I cannot presume it to be unseasonable to invite your attention to the advantages of superadding to the means of education provided by the several States, a seminary of learning, instituted by the national legislature ... [it] would be universal in its beneficial effects. By enlightening the opinions, by expanding the patriotism, and by assimilating the principles, the sentiments and the manners of those who might resort to this temple of science, to be redistributed in due time through every part of the community; sources of jealousy and prejudice would be diminished, the features of national character would be multiplied, and greater extent given to social harmony. But above all, a well-constituted seminary ... would contribute not less to strengthen the foundations, than to adorn the structure of our free and happy system of government.*[37]

More pressing international events again derailed Madison's efforts on behalf of public education. The onset of the War of 1812, coupled with the burning of the nation's capital by the British, prevented the measure from becoming law. This failure, however, did nothing to lessen Madison's fundamental belief in the importance of education and the advancement of knowledge, both necessary for the health and well-being of the nation. He astutely observed, "A popular Government without popular information, or the means of acquiring it, is but a Prologue to a Farce or a Tragedy; or, perhaps both."[38]

In 1817, Madison retired from the presidency and formal political life. He returned gladly to Montpelier with his wife, Dolley, openly anticipating the joys of retirement as well as the opportunity to focus his attention on matters of personal priority rather than public want. It would provide the added benefit of allowing him to devote more time to his friendship with Thomas Jefferson, and he became a frequent and welcome visitor, along with Dolley, to Monticello.

With the return to peace and the inauguration of a new president, there came a surge in nationalism, patriotism, and pride throughout the country. Native-born American writers and artists, including James Fenimore Cooper, Washington Irving, and Thomas Cole, celebrated and glorified this time. Thousands of settlers migrated westward with the onset of manifest destiny, and President James Monroe encouraged local manufactures, domestic prosperity, and economic growth. Despite the perceived domestic tranquility, the dangers of sectionalism and political discord had not been altogether eliminated due to the pernicious reality of chattel slavery. Madison's traditional faith, optimism, and vision for the American republic remained steadfast in this new era, however, and he hoped to promote an educated citizenry to protect its continued well-being. Madison became a willing ally of Thomas Jefferson in his efforts to advance the cause of public education in Virginia through the establishment of a new university. Madison wrote of the importance of this mission in 1822.

> *Learned Institutions ought to be favorite objects with every free people. They throw that light over the public mind which is the best security against crafty & dangerous encroachments on the public liberty. They are the nurseries of skilful Teachers for the schools distributed throughout the Community … They multiply the educated individuals from among whom the people may elect a due portion of their public Agents.*[39]

The proposed university that Jefferson and Madison favored would have no affiliation with any religious sect. It would be dedicated to what Jefferson referred to as "the illimitable freedom of the human mind"[40] and a bastion of enlightenment principles.

Through his masterful skill and creativity as a mathematician, Jefferson was able to convince the Virginia state legislature to finance the proposed college in Charlottesville. His cryptic calculations allegedly proved his hometown to be the geographical and demographic center of the state. A governing board of trustees was formed that included three American presidents—Jefferson, Madison, and Monroe. Meetings of this governing board were held with regularity at both Monticello and Montpelier to plan the curricula and hire the professors. The college was conceived with a firm conviction in the importance of institutionalizing the doctrine of separation of church and state. The university thus acquired a strong secular nature that alarmed many in the community who feared it would be openly hostile to established religion. Madison assured the critics of the university that "with professorships of rival sects, it would be an Arena of theological Gladiators" with open debate and freedom of discussion.[42] Moreover, Madison noted, "although Theology was not to be taught at the University, its Library ought to contain pretty full information for such as might voluntarily seek it in that branch of learning."[43] This opportunity for free inquiry, Madison hoped, would enable students to develop their own religious principles and faith without coercion or compulsion.

Construction of what Jefferson referred to as his "academical village" began on October 6, 1817, with a ceremonial laying of the cornerstone for the school's first academic structure (Pavilion VII).[44] Jefferson's unique and brilliant architectural plan called for the central feature of the campus to be the Rotunda, which housed the brain of the university—the library. After finally securing funding from the state legislature, which had balked at the cost of this "extravagance," work began in 1823 and proceeded hastily to prevent the lawmakers from changing their minds. The Rotunda was modeled in scale after the Pantheon in Rome, certainly the best-

UNIVERSITY OF VIRGINIA LIBRARY

An early representation of the Lawn at the University of Virginia. James Madison was a strong advocate of education and served on the university's board of visitors. He was appointed the school's rector after Thomas Jefferson's death in 1826. Madison maintained that "learned Institutions ought to be favorite objects with every free people. They throw that light over the public mind which is the best security against crafty and dangerous encroachments on the public liberty."

preserved structure from classical antiquity. Jefferson's domed structure was built of brick, comprising a perfect geometric circle, and was, in Jefferson's words, intended "to give [the university's grounds] unity and consolidation as a single object."[45]

The student dormitories, classrooms, and professors' residences constituted the remainder of the university. Built in two parallel wings, east and west lawn, they emanated outward from the Rotunda in a horseshoe fashion with an open vista to the southwest. There were fifty-four student rooms protected by a covered walkway that featured 206 Doric columns, literally a visual essay on architecture.[46] Interspersed at regular intervals were ten, two-story pavilions that served the dual function of classrooms and housing for the faculty. Jefferson's bold concept was for both teachers and students to live together and freely intermingle in their daily pursuit of truth, knowledge, and virtue. This innovative idea reflected Jefferson's unrepentant idealism as well as his belief that a university would be a noble place of learning, where the quest for wisdom would be supreme. In effect, he was creating an American version of the Greek agora. John Adams, although skeptical of the college's ultimate success, was impressed by Jefferson's vision and wrote to him, "I congratulate you and Madison and Monroe on your noble employment in founding a university. From such a noble triumvirate, the world will expect something very great and very new."[47]

The first students arrived at the university in 1825 and quickly destroyed Jefferson's utopian vision for the school. Most of the young men failed to meet even a minimal expectation for scholarship, and Jefferson was forced to acknowledge that about one-third of them were nothing more than "idle ramblers."[48] In October, a group of drunk and disorderly students disguised themselves as Indians and threw a bottle of urine (or some other foul-smelling fluid) through one of the professor's windows. The following night, the disorders on the Lawn continued; when two of the professors ventured out to confront the rowdy students, they were verbally insulted and pelted with sticks and other convenient objects. Thomas Jefferson recounted the incident in a letter written in October 1825.

> *The University had gone on with a degree of order and harmony which had strengthened the hope that much of self government might be trusted to the discretion of students . . . until the 1ˢᵗ instant in the night of that day a party of 14 students, animated first with wine, masked themselves so as not to be known, and turned out on the lawn of the University, with no intention, it is believed but childish noise and uproar. Two Professors hearing it went out to see what was the matter. They were received with insult, and even brick bats were thrown at them.*

Each of them seized an offender, demanded their names (for they could not distin-
guish them under their disguises) but were refused, abused and the culprits calling
on their companions for rescue got loose and withdrew to the chambers.[49]

The faculty was rightfully incensed and demanded that Jefferson and the Board
of Visitors do something immediately about the inappropriate behavior. When
informed of the turmoil at the university, Jefferson was forced to make the strenu-
ous ride down from his mountaintop home to the city despite his feeble and rapidly deteriorating health. He convened an emergency session of the trustees to
deal with the troubles. With both James Madison and James Monroe at his side,
Thomas Jefferson—renowned author of the Declaration of Independence and distinguished third President of the United States—confronted the offending students with their misconduct. He was too overcome with emotion and unable to
speak, as one of the offending students would later recall the dramatic scene. "At a
long table near the center of the room sat the most august body of men I had ever
seen—Jefferson, Madison and Monroe. . . . Jefferson arose to address the students.
He began by declaring that it was one of the most painful events of his life, but he
had not gone far before his feelings overcame him, and he sat down."[50] Jefferson
ultimately accepted the recommendations from the board to impose new, strict
regulations governing student behavior. Among them, according to author Pendleton Hogan, "Students must be in bed by 9:00 PM, rise at dawn, breakfast by
candlelight, and wear a dull gray uniform. No student could own a gun, a horse,
or a dog. Smoking, gambling, and drinking were forbidden."[51] Jennings Wagoner
explains further in his article, "Honor and Dishonor."

[Jefferson] lived long enough to see his idealistic theory of student honor badly
tarnished. Before he died in the summer of 1826, he had witnessed not only the
eruption of some 'vicious irregularities,' but had to face the consequences of the
first of what proved to be a series of riots or rebellions at the university.[52]

Over the next few months, Jefferson and Madison corresponded with their
usual regularity, mostly concerning routine matters involving the university. In
February 1826, however, Jefferson's letter to Madison ended poignantly. Obvi-
ously aware that his own life was nearing an end, Jefferson confided to Madison,
"It is a comfort to leave that institution under your care . . . To myself you have
been a pillar of support through life. Take care of me when dead, and be assured
that I shall leave with you my last affections."[53] The remaining few letters that
were exchanged between these great men were unremarkable.

Madison and Jefferson were destined to meet personally one last time in April 1826 at the regular Board of Visitors meeting in Charlottesville. Upon learning of Jefferson's death some three months later, Madison became the rector of the University of Virginia. For the next eight years, he served with distinction, hiring new faculty members, expanding course offerings, and enlarging the library to more than 10,000 volumes. By 1834, though, Madison's own health was failing, and he was becoming increasingly immobile, unable to make the trip to Charlottesville. He resigned his position as rector content in the legacy he had left in education. As he had written sometime earlier,

What spectacle can be more edifying or more seasonable, than that of liberty & learning, each leaning on the other for their mutual & surest support?[54]

ENDNOTES

Epigraph: John Pendleton Kennedy quoted in Drew R. McCoy, *The Last of the Fathers: James Madison & the Republican Legacy* (Cambridge: Cambridge University Press, 1998), 17.

[1] At the time of Madison's birth, because of the Protestant Reformation and Protestants' fierce opposition to the papacy, the British were still using the inaccurate Julian calendar. As a result, Madison's birth is sometimes recorded as March 5, 1750 (OS), but it was, in fact, March 16, 1751, according to the Gregorian calendar.

[2] James I quoted in Eric Burns, *The Smoke of the Gods: A Social History of Tobacco* (Philadelphia: Temple University Press, 2007), 46.

[3] Virginia has an excellent series of navigable rivers—the James, the York, the Rappahannock, and the Potomac. These rivers divide the state's tidewater region into three peninsulas—the lower peninsula (between the James and York rivers), the middle peninsula (between the York and Rappahannock rivers), and the Northern Neck (between the Rappahannock and Potomac rivers). Virginia has four distinct geographical regions—tidewater, the piedmont, the Shenandoah Valley, and the mountain west.

[4] The fall line of the James is at Richmond; the Rappahannock cataracts are at Fredericksburg; the Potomac's are at Alexandria/Washington, D.C.

[5] At his death, Ambrose Madison listed ownership of twenty-nine slaves. See Ann L. Miller, *The Short Life and Strange Death of Ambrose Madison* (Orange: Orange County Historical Society, 2001), 28. See also Beth Taylor, "James Madison and Slavery" (lecture presented at James Madison University, 2008).

[6] Oyer and Terminer trial quoted in Douglas B. Chambers, *Murder at Montpelier: Igbo Africans in Virginia* (Jackson: University Press of Mississippi, 2005), 5.

[7] Miller, *Death of Ambrose Madison*, 27-28. The accused slaves were Pompey, Turk, and Dido. Pompey was the person executed.

[8] In one of history's interesting coincidences, John Wilkes Booth crossed the Rappahannock River at the ferry crossing between Port Conway and Port Royal in April 1865 after having assassinated President Abraham Lincoln. Booth was killed a short time later at the Garrett farm house a short distance away. Today, Port Royal is in slow but consistent decay, but its eighteenth century architecture is readily apparent. See http://www.co.caroline.va.us/portroyal.html.

[9] Nelly's mother, Rebecca Catlett Conway, had remarried at this point. William T. Hutchinson, ed., *Papers of James Madison 16 March 1751-16 December 1779* (Chicago: University of Chicago Press, 1962), 3.

[10] Only two of Madison's eleven siblings would out live him—William Madison (1762-1843) and Sarah Catlett (1764-1843).

[11] Bryan Green, Ann L. Miller, and Conover Hunt, *Building a President's House: The Construction of James Madison's Montpelier*, (Orange: The Montpelier Foundation, 2007), 5.

[12] Madison quoted in Douglass Adair, "James Madison's Autobiography," *The William and Mary Quarterly 2*, no. 2 (1945): 197. Donald Robertson lived from 1717 until 1783.

[13] The Mattaponi and the Pamunkey Rivers are tributaries of the York. Todd's Bridge was a major tobacco warehouse on the river south of Robertson's school. Robinson Daingerfeld operated it for the merchants McCall and Elliot of Glasgow.

[14] Elizabeth S. Gray, "Donald Robertson and His School in King and Queen County," *The Bulletin of the King and Queen County Historical Society of Virginia 14*, 2. Today, nothing remains of Robertson's school, and the site is overgrown with trees and vegetation.

[15] Douglas Adair quoted in Willard Thorp, *The Lives of Eighteen from Princeton* (Princeton: Princeton University Press, 1946), 139. Robertson's influence on his students was considerable. According to J. Handly Wright, "Attesting to the quality of both the student body and the instruction, the Robertson school turned out one President of the United States, two Virginia Governors, the father of another president, a Naval hero, a father of a United States Supreme Court Justice, a signer of the Declaration of Independence, and several senior officers in the War for American Independence." See Wright, "The Remarkable Scholars of Donald Robertson," *The Bulletin of the King and Queen Historical Society.*

[16] Hutchinson, *Papers of James Madison 16 March 1751-16 December 1779*, 5. Apparently, Madison spoke French with a Scottish accent, which made him difficult to understand.

[17] David Mays quoted in Gray, "Donald Robertson and His School in King and Queen County," *The Bulletin of the King and Queen County Historical Society of Virginia 14*, 2-6 (1963): 5.

[18] Donald Robertson died on January 30, 1783. According to his descendants, he was informed that day of the ratification of the Treaty of Paris ending the Revolutionary War. "His joy and gratitude over this intelligence were unbounded, and he remarked, 'This is the end for which I have longed and prayed. Having lived to see the independence of my country established, I am now satisfied.' Then expressing weariness, he went into his bedroom and lay down. Shortly thereafter one of the family followed him and discovered him lying dead upon his bed." William Kyle Anderson, *Donald Robertson and His Wife Rachel Rogers* (self-published manuscript, 1900), 23. Rachel Rogers Robertson lived on the estate with her two surviving children, Lucy and Isaac, until her death in 1792. Lucy abandoned the homestead and moved to Kentucky while Isaac was enrolled at Princeton. Where the Robertsons are buried is uncertain, but they most likely were interred at the Saint David's Church (sometimes referred to as the Cattail Church) in Aylett. There are no existing markers.

[19] There were only eight colleges in the colonies at the time of the American Revolution: Harvard, the College of William and Mary, Yale University, the University of Pennsylvania, the College of New Jersey (Princeton), King's College (Columbia), the College of Rhode Island (Brown University), Queen's College (Rutgers), and Dartmouth. Only William and Mary was in the south.

[20] There were some outstanding faculty members at the college, including George Wythe and William Small. Madison's cousin, the Reverend James Madison, was also an instructor at William and Mary and later became the institution's eighth president.

[21] Philip Fithian quoted in Hunter Dickenson Farish, ed., *Journal and Letters of Philip Vickers Fithian: A Plantation Tutor of the Old Dominion, 1773-1774* (Charlottesville: University Press of Virginia, 1983), 65. Fithian's journal is a delightful and revealing glimpse into life in colonial Virginia.

[22] Madison quoted in Adair, 197.

[23] Ralph Ketcham, *James Madison: A Biography* (Charlottesville: University of Virginia Press, 1990), 27.

[24] Madison to the Reverend Thomas Martin, August 10, 1769, in Hutchinson, *Papers of James Madison 16 March 1751-16 December 1779*, 43. This is the first letter from James Madison that is known to exist.

[25] M.D. Peterson, ed., *James Madison: A Biography in His Own Words*, The Founding Fathers series (New York: Newsweek, 1974), 20.

[26] William Bradford to James Madison, March 1, 1773, in Hutchinson, *Papers of James Madison 16 March 1751-16 December 1779*, 80.

[27] Madison to William Bradford, July 1, 1774, in Hutchinson, *Papers of James Madison 16 March 1751-16 December 1779*, 114.

[28] Madison to William Bradford, November 9, 1772, in Hutchinson, *Papers of James Madison 16 March 1751-16 December 1779*, 74.

[29] William Bradford to James Madison, October 13, 1772, in Hutchinson, *Papers of James Madison 16 March 1751-16 December 1779*, 72-73.

[30] Madison to William Bradford, June 19, 1775, in Hutchinson, *Papers of James Madison 16 March 1751-16 December 1779*, 153.

[31] Many of Madison's contemporaries, including John Marshall, James Monroe, and Alexander Hamilton, served with distinction in the Continental Army.

[32] Madison to William Barry, August 4, 1822, in Jack Rakove, *James Madison Writings* (New York, Penguin Press, 1999), 791.

[33] Thomas Jefferson to P. J. duPont, April 24, 1816. Available at http://odur.let.rug.nl/~usa/P/tj3/writings/brf/jefl243.htm.

[34] George Washington's Eighth Annual Message to Congress, December 7, 1796. Available at http://www.yale.edu/lawweb/avalon/presiden/sou/washs08.htm

[35] Ibid.

[36] Madison quoted in Philip Bigler, "The Power Which Knowledge Gives," *Madison, the James Madison University Magazine 29, no.3 (2006)*: 40. Available at http://www.jmu.edu/madisononline/madison/2006-Summer.shtml. George Washington was keenly aware of his lack of formal education.

[37] Ibid., 40.

[38] Madison quoted in James Morton Smith, 1821.

[39] Madison to William Barry, August 4, 1822, in Rakove, *Writings*, 791.

[40] Thomas Jefferson quoted at http://www.monticello.org/reports/quotes/uva.html.

[41] Thomas Jefferson to P. J. duPont, April 24, 1816. Available at http://odur.let.rug.nl/~usa/P/tj3/writings/brf/jefl243.htm.

[42] Madison quoted in Ketcham, *James Madison: A Biography* (Charlottesville: University of Virginia Press, 1990) 652.

[43] Ibid., 652.

[44] Alan Pell Crawford, *Twilight at Monticello*: *The Final Years of Thomas Jefferson* (New York: Random House, 2008), 150, 152.

[45] Thomas Jefferson quoted in James Morton Smith, 1819-1820.

[46] To live on the Lawn is considered the supreme honor for University of Virginia students. Previous residents have included Edgar Allan Poe, Woodrow Wilson, Ralph Sampson, and Katie Couric. The University's website notes: "It is considered an honor at the University to live in one of the prestigious Lawn rooms. Located in Mr. Jefferson's original buildings, these rooms are truly in the center of the University. The setting is the beautiful Lawn, probably the most popular place for students to relax, study, and play. There are rooms for 104 students. Living on the Lawn is restricted to undergraduate degree applicants in their final year of study at the University. The rooms are furnished with a bed, desk, wardrobe, bookcase, rocking chair, and blinds on the windows. Additionally, most rooms have a fireplace. No air conditioning, kitchen, computer rooms or study lounges are available; however, students can find whatever is needed just a few steps from their doors." See the Housing Division of the University of Virginia's Web site at: http://www.virginia.edu/housing/options.php?id=lawn&type=transfer.

[47] John Adams quoted in Garry Wills, *Mr. Jefferson's University* (Washington, D.C., National Geographic Society, 2002), 141.

[48] Thomas Jefferson quoted in Dumas Malone, *Jefferson and His Time: The Sage of Monticello* (Boston, Little, Brown and Company, 1981), 1919.

[49] Thomas Jefferson to Joseph Coolidge, October 13, 1825, available on Microfilm, The Jefferson Papers of the University of Virginia 1732-1828 Main Series III.

[50] Henry Tutwiler quoted in James Morton Smith, 1920.

[51] Pendleton Hogan, *The Lawn: A Guide to Jefferson's University* (Charlottesville, Rector and Board of Visitors, 1996), 68.

[52] L. Wagoner Jennings, "Honor and Dishonor at Mr. Jefferson's University: The Antebellum Years," *History of Education Quarterly 26*, no. 2, (1986): 175. Jefferson wrote to Joseph Coolidge shortly before his death: "Our University is going on well. The students have sensibly improved since the last year in habits of order and industry. Occasional instances of insubordination have obliged us from time to time to strengthen our regulations to meet new cases. But the most effectual instrument we have found to be the civil authority the terrors of indictment, fine imprisonment binding to the good behavior … I suppose the more easily, as at the age of 16. It is high time for youth to begin to learn and to practice the duties of obedience to the laws of their country." Available on Microfilm The Jefferson Papers of the University of Virginia 1732-1828 Main Series III.

[53] Thomas Jefferson to James Madison, February 17, 1826, in James Morton Smith, 1966-1967. Madison and Jefferson exchanged a few more letters, but they were unremarkable.

[54] Madison to William Barry, August 4, 1822, in Rakove, *Writings*, 791.

CHAPTER THREE

Anglicans, Baptists, and Liberty of Conscience

Madison's reflections seemed to me the most profound, the most weighty, denoting a great mind and a good heart. — COUNT CARLO VIDUA

The jail at Culpepper Courthouse was reserved primarily for petty thieves, common criminals, and other undesirables; but in 1772, two Baptist preachers were incarcerated there as well. Their crimes included preaching too loudly and challenging the recognized authority of the Anglican Church by preaching "Sedition & Stirring up Strife amongst his Majestie's Liege People."[1] The persecution of religious dissenters was widespread throughout the colony of Virginia, and soon even more preachers were being arrested for sermonizing without a license. Others were being publicly humiliated, horsewhipped, "pelted with apples and stone," or imprisoned with "drunken rowdies." Ironically, even such brutal harassment did little to deter the Baptists in their religious fervor, and they continued to preach and testify, sometimes from the confines of their jail cells.[2]

In James Madison's home county of Orange, Baptist sentiment was strong and growing.[3] Having just returned from the far more tolerant and enlightened middle colonies, Madison found the relentless attacks upon religious belief to be unconscionable and in direct violation of all professed principles of individual liberty. In a letter to his friend, William Bradford, in 1774 Madison wrote, "You are happy in dwelling in a Land where those inestimable privileges are fully enjoyed and the public has long felt the good effects of their religious as well as Civil Liberty."⁴ In an earlier letter, he had lamented the climate of intolerance and bigotry in Virginia.

I want again to breathe your free Air. I expect it will mend my Constitution & confirm my principles. I have indeed as good an Atmosphere at home as the Climate will allow: but have nothing to brag of as to the State and Liberty of my Country. Poverty and Luxury prevail among all sorts: Pride ignorance and Knavery among the Priesthood and Vice and Wickedness among the Laity. This is bad enough But It is not the worst I have to tell you. That diabolical Hell conceived principle of persecution rages among some and to their eternal Infamy the Clergy can furnish their Quota of Imps for such business. This vexes me the most of any thing whatever. There are at this [time?] in the adjacent County not less than 5 or 6 well meaning men in close Goal for publishing their religious Sentiments which in the main are very orthodox. I have neither patience to hear talk or think of any thing relative to this matter, for I have squabbled and scolded abused and ridiculed SO long about it, [to so lit]tle purpose that I am without common patience. So I [leave you] to pity me and pray for Liberty of Conscience to revive among us.⁵

Unlike the New England colonies, which had been settled and populated by religious rebels, the prime motivation for Virginia's colonists had been economic. Thus it became a haven for a more secular breed of fortune seekers and adven-

Bruton Parish Church in the capital of Williamsburg. The Anglican Church was a significant part of colonial Virginia society and was supported by public taxes and tithes.

turers. Still, religion played a vital and necessary role in the society. One of the first priorities of the early Jamestown settlers was to construct an Anglican chapel, and they did this within a short time after finishing the settlement's defensive fortifications. Soon, local laws governing the colony required all of the Jamestown settlers to faithfully observe the Sabbath in an effort to impose some semblance of order and discipline as well as to establish a modicum of basic civility.

As Virginia slowly stabilized over the ensuing decades, Sunday services likewise evolved. They still served as an occasion for some weekly spiritual contemplation but with the added benefit of offering an opportunity for planters and their families to gather together with their distant neighbors to conduct business and socialize in what amounted to little more than "a Day of Pleasure & amusements."[6] To a pious Presbyterian tutor, Philip Fithian, in Westmoreland County, this overt lack of religious piety was shocking.

Anglican ministers were keenly aware of the role that the church played in southern civilization, and, as a result, they were necessarily deferential to the wishes and whims of the lay vestry. This governing body of a church consisted of twelve of the parish's most elite gentlemen. According to historian Warren Billings, among the many duties of the vestry, they "recruited ministers, maintained parish property, cared for the infirm and indigent, and prosecuted moral offences in the county courts."[7] Since they also determined the minister's salary, paid in tobacco and with glebe lands due to the lack of a stable currency, an Anglican clergyman needed to be quite careful to avoid offending his congregants. Thus, the sermons in typical Virginia churches were modest, calm, and brief. Philip Fithian again observed with some dismay, "In the Church at Service, prayrs [are] read over in haste, a Sermon seldom under & never over twenty minutes." Establishment Virginians preferred their religion bland and insisted that their ministers not spiritually challenge their consciences (especially in regards to slavery) or to question their less than saintly leisurely pursuits, which included such impious activities as horseracing, gambling, cockfighting, and drinking.

Before the American Revolution, colonial Virginia was a well-defined and predictable society with a clearly evident public hierarchy. There was no modern sense of egalitarianism or infatuation with democracy; instead, all citizens knew and understood their distinct position within an existing social structure.[8] At the very top of the social hierarchy was the gentry class; it consisted of the colony's largest and most prominent plantation owners and was concentrated in the tidewater regions of Virginia. Although relatively few in number, these individuals

considered themselves to be rational believers in the principles of the Enlightenment, and they exerted an enormous influence over virtually all aspects of society, including government, politics, and religion. They were accustomed to leadership roles and were comfortable with both power and privilege. Their tobacco
plantations were, in fact, global conglomerates with property holdings consisting
of thousands of acres of land worked by dozens of field slaves.[9] The manor houses
on these vast estates were consciously designed to reflect the gentry's social standing, prestige, and wealth.

Immediately below the gentry class were the middling planters, a group far
larger in actual numbers. These Virginians were also tobacco farmers and thus
shared a common economic interest with the upper class, but their plantations
were dramatically smaller, their homes modest, and their field tended by just a
few slaves. Their revenue was marginal and unpredictable, subject to the whims
of nature and the volatility of global tobacco prices.

The most rapidly growing portion of Virginia's population in the mid-eigh-
teenth century comprised small, independent farmers.[10] Concentrated in the western portions of the colony, particularly in the piedmont and Shenandoah Valley
regions, these individuals were often recent immigrants to the state (often migrat-
ing south from Pennsylvania) or transplanted settlers from the eastern counties in
search of fresh lands on the frontier. They owned no slaves, but rather depended
upon large families to assist with the growing and harvesting of their crops. They
also constituted a surprising diversity of religious backgrounds that included large
numbers of Lutherans, Presbyterians, Methodists, Mennonites, and Baptists. Jonathan Boucher, an Anglican minister, estimated that there were, at minimum,
sixty-four separate Christian sects within the British Empire alone.[11]

PHILIP BIGLER

The Great House at Stratford Hall in Westmoreland County, Robert E. Lee's boy-
hood home. The landed gentry constituted only a small part of Southern society,
but these large landholders dominated all aspects of political and economic life.

The Scarecrow painted by Allen Carter Redwood. Virginia's plantation economy was based upon tobacco. This labor-intensive crop was cultivated by a large, enslaved population, comprising individuals who were required to toil in the fields from "can see to can't see."

At the very bottom of Virginia's social hierarchy was its massive enslaved population. In 1770, it was estimated that the colony had more than 187,000 slaves, constituting roughly forty percent of the colony's entire population and by far the largest slave population of any of the original thirteen states.[12] These people had no political or legal rights, and their lives consisted of a never-ending, repetitive cycle of physical toil and cruelty.[13] Only on Sunday were slaves given some respite from their lives of continual hard labor. As Philip Fithian noted in his journal, "Generally here by five o-Clock on Saturday every Face (especially the Negroes) looks festive & cheerful—All the lower class of people, & the Servants, & the slaves, consider it as a Day of Pleasure & amusement, & spend it in such Diversions as they severally choose."[14]

Indirectly, the Anglican Church in Virginia supported the established social hierarchy. The church's official canon, the Book of Common Prayer, emphasized obedience to God and monarch thereby implying that there was little room for dissent or unhappiness with one's proscribed social circumstances. The flaw in this logic left the church and the Tidewater gentry ill-prepared for the cataclysmic demographic changes that were sweeping the frontier. In fact, throughout the rural areas of Virginia, there was widespread disillusionment with Anglican ministers who were collectively viewed as corrupt and unresponsive to the peo-

ple's spiritual needs. James Madison noted the growing problem with the Anglican clergy in a letter to Bradford in 1774.

> That liberal catholic and equitable way of thinking as to the rights of Con-
> science, which is one of the Characteristics of a free people and so strongly
> marks the People of your province is but little known among the Zealous
> adherents to our Hierarchy. … the Clergy are a numerous and powerful
> body[,] have great influence at home by reason of their connection with &
> dependence on the Bishops and Crown and will naturally employ all their art
> & Interest to depress their rising Adversaries; for such they must consider dis-
> senters who rob them of the good will of the people and may in time endanger
> their livings & security.[15]

The Baptists posed the clearest and most overt threat to the primacy of the
tidewater aristocracy. These devout and simple people emphasized an individual's
personal relationship with God, thus eliminating any need for ordained clergy as
an intermediary. They also took their religion seriously, practicing full emersion
(or "dipping") adult baptism so that a penitent could be born again in Christ.[16]
Baptist services were emotional and expressive, in marked contrast to the stark
and ritualistic formality of the Anglican faith. Moreover, they could be sponta-
neous and certainly were not confined to the decorous settings of a church on
Sunday mornings. Preaching and testifying happened everywhere and could just
as easily occur under a tree or in an open pasture or in the confines of a jail cell
since the worship of God knew no artificial boundaries. Furthermore, the Baptists were openly evangelical and egalitarian in their beliefs; they made no distinction in social rank or order since everyone was equally a child of God. This
further horrified the planter class and was aggravated by the fact that the Baptists
made direct overtures towards the colony's enslaved population, openly recognizing their humanity for the first time. Perhaps their greatest transgression, though,
was that they self-righteously condemned the many moral vices typical of southern colonial life. As Philip Fithian noted, "[Mr. Lane] thinks [that the Baptists
are] quite destroying pleasure in the Country; for they encourage ardent Pray'r;
strong & constant faith, & an intire Banishment of Gaming, Dancing, & Sab-
bath-Day Diversions."[17] To the Virginia gentry, their transgressions and lapses in
virtue were mere indulgences that allowed them to live a good and enjoyable life
on this earth. James Madison was troubled at the vile reaction by the Virginia
establishment to the Baptists. More importantly, he understood the dire implica-

tions inherent in attempting to restrict any religious belief. Ultimately, he understood, such actions by government could be construed to be an effort to curtail freedom of thought, which was the most essential of all liberties. Madison kept his college friend, William Bradford, well informed of the religious abuses, and Bradford responded in a letter written in 1774.

> *I am sorry to hear that Persecution has got so much footing among you. The description you give of your Country makes me more in love with mine. Indeed I have ever looked on America as the land of freedom when compared with the rest of the world, but compared with the rest of America Tis Pennsylvania that is so. Persecution is a weed that grows not in our happy soil: and I do not remember than an Person was ever imprisoned here for his religious sentiments however heretical or unepiscopal they might be. Liberty is the Genius of Pennsylvania, and its inhabitants think speak and act with a freedom unknown—I do indeed pity you.* [18]

Ironically, it was because of the persecution of the Baptists that Madison discovered his life's first great cause—that of promoting religious liberty. Not coincidentally, he saw the elements of tyranny both behind the maltreatment of the Baptists as well as the current repression being perpetrated by the British against Boston and the rest of the American colonies. As he was increasingly radicalized towards the patriot cause, Madison became more active in local Virginia politics. In 1776, after the hasty and strategic departure of the last royal governor of the colony, Lord Dunmore, Madison was elected to serve as a delegate to the Virginia Convention then being convened in the capital of Williamsburg. As one of the youngest members of this revolutionary body, his role was, inevitably, subordinate to that of the more senior and experienced representatives, something that Madison himself openly acknowledged in his *Autobiographical Notes.* "Being young & in the midst of distinguished and experienced members of the Convention he [Madison] did not enter into its debates; tho' he occasionally suggested amendments."[19] He did, however, receive a choice appointment to serve on a key committee that was chaired by the venerable George Mason of Fairfax County. Its purpose was essentially to draft what would be the philosophical basis for a new, free, and independent government for Virginia.

According to Robert Hawkes, professor emeritus at George Mason University, the genius of George Mason at the Virginia convention was his success in transforming various abstract revolutionary principles into a realistic, prac-

tical, and effective governing philosophy.[20]
Although his committee was massive, consisting of 60 members, Mason took most of
the responsibility for writing the first draft
of what became known as the Virginia Declaration of Rights. This radical document
began by firmly asserting, "That all men are
by nature equally free and independent, and
have certain inherent rights, of which, when
they enter into a state of society, they cannot, by any compact, deprive or divest their
posterity; namely, the enjoyment of life and
liberty, with the means of acquiring and pos-
sessing property, and pursuing and obtain-
ing happiness and safety."[21] These extraor-
dinarily significant words would soon be
slightly altered and transformed by fellow

George Mason of Gunston Hall.
Mason was the primary author of
the Virginia Declaration of Rights.
A young James Madison inserted
key phrasing into this document
that guarantees religious freedom.

Virginian, Thomas Jefferson, into a more articulate manifesto (the Declaration
of Independence) at the Second Continental Congress in Philadelphia.[22]

For James Madison, though, the single most important clause in Mason's
original draft of the document was Article XVI, which dealt with religious
freedom. Mason had initially written "that religion or the duty which we owe
to our CREATOR, and the manner of discharging it, can be governed only
by reason and conviction, not by force or violence; and therefore, that all men
should enjoy the fullest toleration in the exercise of religion, according to the dic-
tates of conscience."[23] Although this appeared at first glance to be an impressive liberalization of Virginia's policies towards religious dissidents, Madison
felt strongly that the word "toleration" could be easily misconstrued and would
eventually be misinterpreted to allow for further mischief against religious dissenters. He proposed a small but substantive change to the document, altering the text to read, "All men *are equally entitled to the free exercise* of religion." This was no mere exercise in semantics, for Madison's amendment established the fundamental principle that religion was exclusively a matter of personal conviction and could not be compelled by any civil government.[24] For
the young James Madison, his first foray into the political realm resulted in an
impressive and substantive philosophical triumph.

Shortly thereafter, Madison was a logical choice to serve in the new Virginia House of Delegates, and he was duly elected by the citizens of Orange County. His tenure was brief, however, since he lost his first bid for re-election the very next year. Early political elections in colonial America were not just an exercise of civic virtue, but were important social occasions as well, with all voting done openly at the local courthouse without the benefit of a secret ballot. It was traditional for the various political candidates to offer ample alcoholic inducements to the voters, but this mercenary practice was contrary to Madison's rapidly evolving republican ideology. He believed, somewhat naïvely, that individual merit and personal virtue should be the foremost qualifications for public office, and that the voters would select the candidate who best exemplified such ideals. Years later, in his autobiography, Madison lamented the corrupt voting practices.

> ... as there the usage for the candidates to recommend themselves to the voters, not only by personal solicitation, but by the corrupting influence of spirituous liquors, and other treats, having a like tendency. Regarding these as equally inconsistent with the purity of moral and of republican principles; and anxious to promote, by his example, the proper reform, he [Madison] trusted to the new views of the subject which he hoped would prevail with the people; whilst his competitors adhered to the old practice.[25]

It was a painful lesson into the more pedestrian aspects of human nature and one that Madison would not forget years later while crafting a new government for the United States of America.

Madison's stinging electoral defeat also threatened to deprive the fledgling Virginia government of James Madison's considerable talents during a time of war. An alternative public office had to be quickly found, so, in 1779, Madison was appointed to serve on the unelected Governor's Council, where he became a key advisor and close friend to the governor, Thomas Jefferson.[26] After a brief interlude in Williamsburg, though, Madison was appointed to serve as one of Virginia's representatives to the Confederation Congress in Philadelphia. He would hold this position over the next three critical years, until his term expired in 1783.[27]

Madison returned to his home at Montpelier and was almost immediately elected again to the state legislature. The Virginia House of Delegates was considered to be a far more significant governmental body than the Confederation Congress, since under the provisions of the nation's first constitution, the vast majority of power was still retained by the states. As the most populous and influential of the original thirteen states, Virginia's legislature was, by far, the most prestigious representative assembly in the United States.

With independence from Great Britain finally secured through the ratification of the Treaty of Paris in 1783, domestic concerns once again became more prominent. Many Virginians were appalled by what was generally perceived to be a lack of civic virtue among their citizens. There was a widespread consensus that this problem was caused by the growing secularization of society and the resulting moral laxity. To compensate, a seemingly minor and innocuous piece of legislation was introduced in the state legislature to authorize the government to financially support "Teachers of the Christian Religion." The bill was well intentioned, outwardly benign, and enjoyed the strong support of Patrick Henry. It seemed predestined to be enacted into law without either much discussion or debate. For James Madison, though, the legislation was a violation of the fundamental principle of religious freedom that had been codified in the Virginia Declaration of Rights. Madison believed that no one should be compelled by a secular or ecclesiastical power to support any religious theology. Left unchallenged, the law would establish a dangerous precedent that would allow the government to intrude at will into what were essentially matters of personal belief. The potential for future mischief was great, Madison warned. "It is proper to take alarm at the first experiment in our liberties ... The freemen of America did not wait till usurped power had strengthened itself by exercise ... They saw all the consequences in the principle, and they avoided the consequences by denying the principle. We revere this lesson too much, soon to forget it."[28] Madison found a willing and able ally in his old mentor, the curmudgeonly George Mason of Gunston Hall. Mason not only agreed philosophically, but also had a general aversion to all forms of taxation.[29]

During this critical time, Madison remained in frequent correspondence with his good friend, Thomas Jefferson, who was serving abroad as American minister to France. Jefferson, an equally outspoken advocate of the separation of church and state, was predictably outraged that the battle for freedom of conscience had to be waged once again. In a private letter to Madison, Jefferson offered a surprisingly candid appraisal of the situation, blaming Patrick Henry for causing the political morass.

> *While Mr. Henry lives another bad constitution would be formed, and saddled for ever on us. What we have to do I think is devoutly to pray for his death, in the mean time to keep alive the idea that the present is but an ordinance and*

*prepare the minds of the young men. I am glad the Episcopalians have again
shewn their teeth and fangs. The dissenters had almost forgotten them.*[30]

Despite Jefferson's peculiar desire that Henry be removed from the state legislature by divine intervention, the far more pragmatic Madison orchestrated an equally effective, albeit more subtle, scheme to reduce Henry's influence within the state. Through clandestine maneuvering, Madison helped elect Henry governor and thus removed the great orator from the debates in the state legislature. Henry proudly assumed his new office, leaving the assessment legislation in hands less able to manage the growing opposition from the Baptists and other religious minorities.

In an era when communication was primitive, letter-writing expensive, and information undependable, the most effective way for citizens to seek redress for their grievances was through formal petition.[31] Madison wrote and circulated what became known as "The Memorial and Remonstrance" for the citizens of Orange County, although he would not publicly acknowledge authorship for decades. Ultimately, fifteen of these petitions protesting the plan for government funding for religious teachers circulated throughout the state and garnered an impressive 1,552 signatures.[32]

"The Memorial and Remonstrance" remains the single-greatest justification for religious liberty in American history. The logic contained within the document is unassailable, and Madison's arguments are persuasive and eloquent. He steadfastly maintained that the way a person chooses to worship God was a matter of personal conscience and could be "directed only by reason and conviction."[33] Thus, any effort by a government to either sanction or prohibit religious beliefs was, in fact, an essential act of tyranny.

The memorial further asserted that individuals had a fundamental right not to believe in any theology and could not be compelled to accept the legitimacy of a given church. Individuals could not be forced to tithe or financially support any religious denomination that they did not voluntarily accept as true.

> *Whilst we assert for ourselves a freedom to embrace, to profess and to observe
> the Religion which we believe to be of divine origin, we cannot deny an equal
> freedom to those whose minds have not yet yielded to the evidence which has
> convinced us. If this freedom be abused, it is an offence against God, not against
> man: To God, therefore, not to man, must an account of it be rendered.*[34]

Thomas Jefferson had offered a similar assessment in his *Notes on the State of Virginia*, claiming that a person's religious beliefs were wholly outside of the public forum. "But it does me no injury for my neighbor to say there are twenty gods or no God. It neither picks my pocket nor breaks my leg."[35]

The Memorial consisted of fifteen paragraphs and concluded with a firm statement.

> *We the Subscribers say, that the General Assembly of this Commonwealth have no such authority: And that no effort may be omitted on our part against so dangerous an usurpation, we oppose to it, this remonstrance; earnestly praying, as we are in duty bound, that the Supreme Lawgiver of the Universe, by illuminating those to whom it is addressed, may on the one hand, turn their Councils from every act which would affront his holy prerogative, or violate the trust committed to them: and on the other, guide them into every measure which may be worthy of his blessing, may redound to their own praise, and may establish more firmly the liberties, the prosperity and the happiness of the Commonwealth.*[36]

Through Madison's efforts, the assessment bill was voted down in the legislature, and its defeat provided the opportunity to resurrect Thomas Jefferson's Statute for Religious Freedom, which had been tabled since 1779. The legislation passed the General Assembly quickly, and James Madison proudly informed Jefferson, "I flatter myself [to] have in this country extinguished forever the ambitious hope of making laws for the human mind."[37] These same sentiments would be later codified into federal law with the adoption of the First Amendment to the Constitution in 1791.

To Madison, Jefferson, and the other founders, religion was an intensely personal matter. Although secular government had no role in supporting or advancing religion, Madison felt that it was "essential to the moral order of the World and to the happiness of man."[38] Moreover, in a letter written in 1822, Madison maintained that "religion flourishes in greater purity, without than with the aid of Govt."[39] Through Madison's efforts, religious liberty in the United States is a fundamental right, and the way, whether, and how one chooses to worship God is essentially an act of faith, a personal choice, and not one of statute.

ENDNOTES

Epigraph: Count Carlo Vidua quoted in James Morton Smith, 11.

[1] Steven Waldman, *Founding Faith: Providence, Politics, and the Birth of Religious Freedom in America* (New York: Random House, 2008), 102-103.

[2] See "The Baptist Index: Outline of Baptist Persecution in Colonial America" at http://www.bruce-gourley.com/Baptists/persecutionoutline.htm.

[3] Warren M. Billings, John Selby, and Thad Tate, *Colonial Virginia: A History* (White Plains: KTO Press, 1986), 323.

[4] Madison to William Bradford, April 1, 1774, in Hutchinson, *Papers of James Madison 16 March 1751-16 December 1779,* 112.

[5] Madison to William Bradford, January 24, 1774, in Hutchinson, *Papers of James Madison 16 March 1751-16 December 1779,* 106

[6] Philip Fithian and James Madison were classmates at Princeton. Philip Fithian quoted in Farish, 137. Ideally, Anglican Churches were located at six-mile intervals throughout the colony, an easy ride for most planters. David Holmes, "Jefferson and Religion" (lecture presented at Monticello-Stratford Seminar, Ash Lawn, Virginia, 2008).

[7] Billings, Selby, and Tate, 65.

[8] Historian Rhys Isaac has written extensively on the nature of Virginia society. His landmark book, *Transformation of Virginia 1740-1790,* was published in 1983 and won the Pulitzer Prize for history. It is still widely read.

[9] The consignment system in Virginia required planters to send their tobacco crops to England, where a merchant would arrange for its sale.

[10] Thomas Jefferson would glorify this group as the mythical "agrarian farmer." He believed that by owning their own land, they would be self-sufficient and virtuous.

[11] Frank Lambert, *The Founding Fathers and the Place of Religion in America* (Princeton: Princeton University Press, 2003), 231.

[12] In fact, Virginia had almost three times the number of slaves of any colony in America. Interestingly, slavery was legal in all of the thirteen colonies, with New York and New Jersey having sizeable slave populations prior to the American Revolution.

[13] In "African Americans on the Move: A Look at Forced and Voluntary Movement of Blacks within America," Kindred Trails Worldwide Genealogy Resources historian Rickie Lazzerini describes the conditions of slave life in the South at http://www.kindredtrails.com/African-Americans-On-The-Move-1.html.

[14] Philip Fithian quoted in Farish, 137.

[15] Madison to William Bradford, April 1, 1774, in Hutchinson, *Papers of James Madison 16 March 1751-16 December 1779,* 112

[16] Virginius Dabney, *Virginia, the New Dominion: A History from 1607 to Present* (Garden City: Doubleday and Company Inc., 1971), 161.

[17] Philip Fithian quoted in Farish, 72.

[18] William Bradford to James Madison, March 4, 1774, in Hutchinson, *Papers of James Madison 16 March 1751-16 December 1779,* 109

[19] Madison quoted in Peterson, 31.

[20] Bob Hawkes was a beloved history professor at George Mason University in Fairfax County, Virginia. His lectures on Mason were always humorous, informative, and inspirational. He was a visiting scholar with the Monticello-Stratford Seminar for Teachers for many years. He died in 2008.

[21] See the Virginia Declaration of Rights at the Avalon Project, available at http://www.yale.edu/lawweb/avalon/virginia.htm.

[22] The ideas and philosophy contained in the Declaration of Independence were widely held and expressed by the patriot elite. The genius of Jefferson was the eloquence of his writing and the clarity he provided to the cause of independence. It is rightfully considered to be a cornerstone document of the American republic.

[23] George Mason's Virginia Declaration of Rights quoted in Vincent Phillip Muñoz, "James Madison's Principle of Religious Liberty," *The American Political Science Review 97,* no. 1 (2003): 24.

[24] Waldman, 114-115.

[25] Madison quoted in Peterson, 42.

[26] Madison first met Jefferson in 1776, but their friendship dates to 1779, while Jefferson was serving as

governor of the Commonwealth of Virginia.

[27] The Articles of Confederation required a forced rotation of office for representatives. It dictated: "No State shall be represented in Congress by less than two, nor more than seven members; and no person shall be capable of being a delegate for more than three years in any term of six years." See the Articles of Confederation at the Avalon Project: http://www.yale.edu/lawweb/avalon/artconf.htm.

[28] Madison quoted in Irving Brant, "Madison: On the Separation of Church and State." *The William and Mary Quarterly 8,* no. 1 (1951): 10.

[29] The power to tax was seen in the colonial period as the power to destroy. The bill levied a tax equal to that of the Tea Act, which had led to the Boston Tea Party and directly to the American Revolution.

[30] Thomas Jefferson to James Madison, December 8, 1784, in James Morton Smith, 351-352.

[31] The fundamental right to petition the government is codified in the First Amendment to the Constitution. Although this may today seem anachronistic, it was an important guarantee in the eighteenth century.

[32] Robert A. Rutland, ed., *The Papers of James Madison: 10 March 1784-28 March 1786,* Chicago: University of Chicago Press, 1973, 297.

[33] Madison's *Memorial and Remonstrance Against Religious Assessments* is available at http://etext.lib. virginia.edu/toc/modeng/public/MadMemo.html.

[34] Ibid.

[35] Thomas Jefferson, *Notes on the State of Virginia,* available at http://etext.lib.virginia.edu/toc/modeng/ public/JefVirg.html.

[36] *Memorial and Remonstrance.*

[37] Madison to Thomas Jefferson, January 22, 1786, in James Morton Smith, 403.

[38] Madison quoted in Waldman, 99.

[39] Madison to Edward Livingston, July 10, 1822, Rakove, *Madison Writings,* 788-789.

James Madison
March 16, 1751 – June 28, 1836

1

An artist's rendition of the original Mount Pleasant estate. Madison's grandfather, Ambrose, established the tobacco plantation in the Virginia Piedmont during the 1720s. Shortly after he relocated his family to the farm, he allegedly was poisoned by slaves and died on August 27, 1732. His widow ran the plantation until her son, James Madison Sr., reached maturity.

Donald Robertson's account book and journal records a 1766 payment of £5 for the young James Madison's schooling. Madison attended Robertson's school in King and Queen County for five years and would later say of his first teacher, "All that I have been in my life, I owe largely to that man."

PHILIP BIGLER

The Lawn at the University of Virginia. James Madison believed that "Learned Institutions ought to be favorite objects with every free people." He devoted much of his retirement to advancing education by working with his close friend, Thomas Jefferson, to establish the University of Virginia in Charlottesville.

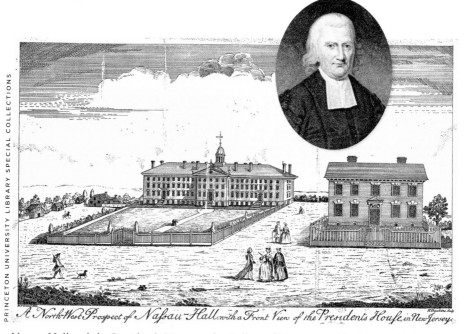

PRINCETON UNIVERSITY LIBRARY SPECIAL COLLECTIONS

Nassau Hall and the President's House at the College of New Jersey. Madison studied under the Reverend Jonathan Witherspoon, and it was here that he developed his lifelong commitment to freedom of religion and a dedication to scholarly studies.

Voting Record for the Constitutional Convention. The Constitution was "unanimously agreed to" on September 17, 1787. Rhode Island did not attend the convention. Two Virginians, Edmund Randolph and George Mason, refused to sign the document because it lacked a definitive Bill of Rights. Elbridge Gerry of Massachusetts also declined to sign.

NATIONAL ARCHIVES

LIBRARY OF CONGRESS

Federal Hall in New York City. The first capital of the United States under the Constitution was New York City. The entire government was housed in Federal Hall, which was located at 26 Wall Street. The capital was moved temporarily to Philadelphia in 1790 and then permanently relocated in 1800 to Washington, D.C.

Signing of the Constitution by Howard Chandler Christy. Painted in 1939, Alexander Hamilton, Benjamin Franklin, and James Madison appear in the center of the picture. The president of the convention, General George Washington, presides.

A typical tobacco field in the South. Tobacco was the cash crop of Virginia, and virtually all land-owners grew the plant, which was extremely labor intensive. The wealth of landowners was determined not by acreage owned, but rather by the quantity of labor available to cultivate the land.

Tobacco drying in a barn. Madison owned approximately one hundred slaves at any given time. Despite the growing anti-slavery sentiment in the country, he was unable to find what he considered a realistic dissolution of the system. He recognized its intrinsic evil, but failed to emancipate any slaves upon his death.

PHILIP BIGLER

The restored Gilmore Cabin at Montpelier. This house was the home of George Gilmore, a Madison slave who was emancipated after the Civil War. Located about one mile from the Montpelier mansion, Gilmore and three generations of descendants lived in the cabin until the 1930s. Today it is preserved in honor of the numerous enslaved African-Americans who worked on the plantation.

A

COLORED MAN'S REMINISCENCES

OF

JAMES MADISON.

BY PAUL JENNINGS.

BROOKLYN:
GEORGE C. BEADLE.
1865.

The cover page of Paul Jenning's brief memoir, *A Colored Man's Reminiscences of James Madison*. Paul Jennings was born in 1799 and was James Madison's body servant. He was with Madison when the former president died in 1836. He later accompanied Dolley Madison to Washington, D.C., where he was eventually purchased by Senator Daniel Webster for $120 and given his freedom.

An artist's rendition
of Montpelier as
it appeared during
Madison's lifetime.

PETER W. GAUT

The President's House after being burned during the War of 1812. In 1814, the British routed American forces at the battle of Bladensburg and forced the evacuation of Washington, D.C. The Executive Mansion (the White House) was burned by British soldiers, but not before they looted the residence and enjoyed the dinner that had been prepared for Mr. Madison. Paul Jennings recounted, "When the British did arrive, they ate up the very dinner, and drank the wines, &c., that I had prepared for the President's party."

George Washington by Gilbert Stuart. According to lore, Dolley Madison refused to evacuate the Executive Mansion until she saved this painting, which hung in the East Room. In truth, she directed its removal; but as Paul Jennings recounted, it was actually taken down by the president's gardener and the White House doorkeeper.

THE LIBRARY OF CONGRESS

"The fall of Washington — or Maddy in full flight." This 1814 British cartoon lampooned President James Madison's evacuation of the nation's new capital. He is portrayed as carrying crucial government documents and papers while the city is in flames. Madison was widely criticized for the lack of an effective defense of Washington, D.C.

THE NATIONAL ARCHIVES

James Madison's letter to the president of the Senate on September 17, 1814. Written, ironically, on the twenty-seventh anniversary of the signing of the Constitution, President Madison noted that "the destruction of the Capitol by the Enemy" required the Congress to seek new accommodations in order to convene the legislative branch.

Dolley Payne Madison
May 20, 1768 – July 12, 1849

PHILIP BIGLER

The Public Vault at Congressional Cemetery. After her death in 1849, Dolley Madison's remains were held here for three years. Her body was later moved to the nearby Caustin Vault, where it remained until 1858, when she was finally returned to Montpelier and buried alongside her husband.

PHILIP BIGLER

The interment record for Dolley Madison. It reads, "July 16, 1849: Mrs. Dolly P. Madison Est D to opening and Use of Public Vault for Mrs. Madison $5.00." Dolley Madison's funeral was one of the most elaborate ever to be held in Washington, D.C. During her eulogy, President Zachary Taylor referred to Dolley as the nation's "first lady." She was the first presidential spouse to be so designated.

Students celebrate Constitution Day at James Madison University. JMU is the only four-year institution of higher education in the United States named for James Madison. Each September 17, members of the 1787 Society distribute copies of the Constitution to students to commemorate the signing of the nation's founding document.

Ashley Connelly and Tommy Bluestein hand out materials on the JMU Commons. The 1787 Society serves as an advisory board to the James Madison Center. Students are selected based upon their outstanding academic record and commitment to learning more about the life and times of James Madison.

Whitney Pack presides over the initiation of new 1787 Society members. On Madison's birthday, March 16, the James Madison Center conducts a wreath-laying ceremony at the James Madison statue. New members of the 1787 Society are recognized during the ceremonies.

Jessica Arms receives the Donald Robertson Scholarship from James Madison Center Director, Philip Bigler. Awarded to an outstanding pre-service elementary school teacher, the Donald Robertson Scholarship is given in honor of James Madison's first tutor. Madison called Robertson a man of extensive learning and acknowledged the enormous influence this teacher had on his life.

James Madison University College of Education students visiting Montpelier. As part of their social studies methods class, pre-service teachers learn about the proper procedures for developing an effective field trip by visiting James Madison's home.

SHAY COCHRANE

CHAPTER FOUR

Vices, Rebellion, and Constitution

{His reading and study} surely made Madison the most cosmopolitan statesman never to have quit American shores. Indeed, it was often remarked a few years later that Madison was probably the best-read and best-informed member of the Constitutional Convention. — ADRIENNE KOCH

Just three years since the signing of the Treaty of Paris, which officially ended the American Revolution, the nation's independence was under threat from a post-war economy that was in total shambles. Discontent was rising in all thirteen states, while the Sixth Confederation Congress was safely ensconced in New York City—ineffective, unproductive, and oblivious. Despite the obvious need for serious fiscal and political action, the nation's sole national governing assembly showed a surprising nonchalance, frequently even failing to achieve a simple quorum (the minimum number of delegates necessary to conduct business) because its legislators' attendance at congressional sessions was casual and unpredictable. In Massachusetts, the crisis had finally reached a boiling point, exacerbated by excessively high taxes, farmers' losing their homes, and the lack of a stable currency. To many of the state's citizens, particularly in the westernmost counties, it seemed that their oppressors were no longer residing in London, but rather were domestically born and bred and living in Boston.

Throughout the Commonwealth of Massachusetts in 1786, rebellious mobs acted to close down the state's hated court system, while simultaneously threatening and intimidating lawyers and judges who had callously presided over foreclosures and imprisoned citizens for non-payment of debt. Even more alarming was an unsuccessful effort by a small group of insurgents led by a former captain in the Continental Army, Daniel Shays, to expand the rebellion by seizing the federal arsenal in Springfield. "Mob-ocracy" and chaos reigned throughout the state, leading one prominent statesman, Elbridge Gerry, to note, "The evils we experience flow from the excess of democracy."[1]

In October, "Light Horse Harry" Lee contacted James Madison about the ominous events in Massachusetts. Lee was concerned that "Shays' Rebellion" had the potential to spread to other states, including Virginia. "It is unquestionably true that present appearances portend extensive national calamity," he wrote. "The contagion will spread and may reach Virginia." The weakness of the federal government and its failure to respond were primarily responsible for the continuing hostilities. "The objects of the malcontents are alluring to the vulgar and the impotency of government is rather an encouragement to, than a restraint on, the licentious,"[2] Lee observed.

The imminent threat of anarchy frightened Madison. Securing domestic tranquility and protecting private property were among a government's most basic and fundamental responsibilities, and yet the disorders in Massachusetts led by "internal enemies" threatened the very essence of civil society.[3] If the mob were allowed to use force and coercion, no man or household would be safe. The whim of the masses would effectively replace the rule of law. It was a prescription for a national disaster.

Thomas Jefferson, who was then serving as American minister to France, remained in close correspondence with Madison, who kept him informed about the unfolding events in Massachusetts. While Madison clearly recognized the peril to the existence of the fragile union, Jefferson showed a remarkable proclivity to excuse such radical actions. He wrote to Madison, "I like a little rebellion now and then. It is like a storm in the atmosphere."[4] After the state militia finally suppressed Shays' Rebellion, Jefferson cavalierly dismissed the danger, whimsically writing to Madison, "The late rebellion in Massachusets [sic] has given more alarm than I think it should have done. Calculate that one rebellion in 13 states in the course of 11 years, is but one for each state in a century and a half. No country should be so long without one."[5] He reiterated his astonishing belief in cyclical uprisings in a letter to William Stephens Smith. "What signify a few lives lost in a century or two? The tree of liberty must be refreshed from time to time with the blood of patriots and tyrants. It is its natural manure."[6]

Such observations from afar were wholly out of touch with the serious reality of the American domestic political situation. Madison knew that the internal bedlam was an attestation to the lack of effective governance. The internal disorders were a national disgrace and a delight to the nation's enemies, particularly the British who saw them as evidence that the United States was failing as an independent nation and may yet return to Britannia's empire. Shays' Rebellion, though, did have at least one positive result in that it provided a much-needed catalyst for political change.

Madison had been long aware of the fundamental flaws inherent in the Confederation government. He had already personally served several frustrating terms in Congress as part of the Virginia delegation and was discouraged by the government's structural inefficiency.[7] In September 1786, Madison had optimistically attended the Annapolis Convention, which had been summoned to deal with a wide variety of commercial ailments and to consider reforms of the Articles of Confederation. Despite the obvious need, only five states—Virginia, North Carolina, Delaware, Pennsylvania, and New York—even bothered to show up. Worse, Maryland, the host state, refused to send delegates. The meeting adjourned in abject failure, but the delegates did issue a plaintive call for yet another convention to convene the following year with a mandate "to render the Constitution of the federal government adequate to the exigencies of the Union."[8]

Madison retreated to Montpelier and there used his time to seriously study the problems with the Articles of Confederation. He began assembling dozens of scholarly books on government that had been provided by the crate load from France by his friend, Thomas Jefferson. He scoured each volume for historical precedents and wisdom by which to reform and remedy the current ills that had beset the American system of government. He compiled his notes under the heading: "Ancient and Modern Confederacies."[9] After thirty-nine handwritten pages, sometimes notated in Latin and Greek, Madison concluded that all confederation governments were structurally doomed to failure since they lacked a strong, centralized unifying authority.[10]

The Annapolis fiasco had confirmed for Madison virtually all of his theoretical speculations about the innate weaknesses of confederation governments. With the next convention scheduled to convene in Philadelphia in May 1787, Madison began to conduct additional research in preparation for his participation at this vital meeting. Although never intended for publication, his resulting essay, "Vices of the Political System of the United States," reflected Madison's deliberate and profound analysis about the nature and scope of human government.

In his writings, Madison conceded that the current system of government under the Articles of Confederation had been an utter failure because the Confederation Congress lacked any real power to pass substantive or binding laws. Thus, compliance by the states to congressional requisitions was voluntary and therefore frequently left either ignored or unfulfilled, even during dire times of war or financial crisis. Madison argued that for any statutory law to be effective, a government must have sufficient power to enforce it. "A sanction is essential to the idea of law, as coercion is to that of Government," he explained. "The federal system being destitute of both, wants the great vital principles of a Political Cons[ti]tution."[11]

Madison openly acknowledged that the Articles of Confederation had been created in good faith by well meaning men, but he also recognized that it came "from a mistaken confidence that the justice, the good faith, the honor, the sound policy, of the several legislative assemblies would render superfluous any appeal to the ordinary motives by which the laws secure the obedience of individuals."[12] The idea of voluntary compliance with the law was sheer fancy, since no state legislature would willingly submit to laws imposed by the federal Congress. Sacrifice for the overall general welfare was wishful thinking, Madison thought. "Every general act of the Union must necessarily bear unequally hard on some particular member or members of [the country]."[13]

Under the provisions of the articles, the states retained the vast majority of power, which had the consequence of making the centralized government weak and ineffective. The absence of effective federal power posed a serious threat to the overall health of the nation and even to the individual liberty of its citizens. The various state legislative assemblies were filled with ambitious men who were little more than what Madison derided as "courtiers of popularity." These politicians shamelessly sought to ingratiate themselves with the general population by constantly passing popular laws, but ones of dubious merit. As a result, "every year, almost every session, adds a new volume," Madison noted.[14] These copious and frivolous laws had little to do with the welfare of the people.

> *As far as laws are necessary, to mark with precision the duties of those who are to obey them, and to take from those who are to administer them a discretion, which might be abused, their number is the price of liberty. As far as the laws exceed this limit, they are a nuisance: a nuisance of the most pestilent kind.*[15]

The dangers of a tyranny of the majority were far more likely on the state and local level, where personal interests were far more parochial.

It was during this critical period, immediately prior to the Constitutional Convention, that Madison developed his sophisticated views on the need to create a new, modern republican form of government. It had to be a carefully devised system, through which power would be delegated and diffused, and where elections would "extract from the mass of the Society the purest and noblest characters" who would selflessly serve the public good.[16]

Madison arrived early in Philadelphia on May 5, 1787. He duly noted in his meteorological journal that the temperature that day reached a high of sixty-eight degrees and that the "air [was] thick" and the "sky muddy." Two days later, as he patiently awaited the coming of his fellow delegates, he observed that the "humming birds [were] frequent" and "the wood bine in blossom."[17] The other members of the Virginian delegation, slowed by perilous roads and poor transportation, arrived separately over the ensuing two weeks. They were collectively an impressive assemblage of talent and brilliance. From Gunston Hall in Fairfax County was the author of the Virginia Declaration of Rights, George Mason; from Richmond, came the renowned lawyer and professor, George Wythe; and finally, there was the governor of the commonwealth, Edmund Randolph.[18] The most important delegate from Virginia, George Washington, once again left his peaceful retirement at Mount Vernon to answer his nation's call to duty during a perilous time of crisis.[19] The fame, honor, and dignity of the American Cincinnatus would immediately provide a sense of legitimacy to the convention's proceedings. In a letter to Thomas Jefferson, Madison noted that "Genl. Washington who arrived on Sunday evening amidst the acclamations of the people, as well as more sober marks of the affection and veneration which continues to be felt for his character."[20]

Ultimately, fifty-five men would attend the Philadelphia convention, including Benjamin Franklin and Alexander Hamilton. Some notable absences, however, included Thomas Jefferson and John Adams, who were serving the government abroad. Madison's great concern was the nonattendance of Patrick Henry, who allegedly refused to attend the convention because "he smelt a rat."[21] In an earlier letter to George Washington, Madison had explained that Henry could ultimately become the leader of any opposition that may arise to the convention's final outcome.

I hear from Richmond with much concern that Mr. Henry has positively declined his mission to Philada. Besides the loss of his services on that theatre, there is danger I fear that this step has proceeded from a wish to leave his conduct unfettered on another theatre where the result of the Convention will receive its destiny from his omnipotence.[22]

A quorum was finally achieved on Friday, May 25, when twenty-nine delegates from nine states gathered at the Pennsylvania State House.[23] Notably absent were New Hampshire, Maryland, and Connecticut, but their delegations would eventually arrive. Rhode Island, on the other hand, obstinately refused to participate in any efforts to modify the articles and boycotted the entire convention process.[24]

Delegate Robert Morris began the official business by nominating George Washington to serve as the assembly's president. The motion was quickly seconded and agreed to by unanimous consent.[25] It would be the last time that the delegates would be in complete agreement.

The diminutive James Madison, sitting "in front of the presiding member, with the other members on my right and left hand," recorded it all, taking detailed notes of the proceedings.[26]

INDEPENDENCE NATIONAL HISTORICAL PARK

The Assembly Room at the Pennsylvania State House. Here the delegates to the Constitutional Convention met during the summer of 1787. Eventually fifty-five men would attend the proceedings, during which much of the debate centered around the Virginia Plan written by James Madison and proposed by Governor Edmund Randolph.

The nomination [of George Washington] came with particular grace from Penna. As Doct Franklin alone could have been thought of as a competitor. The Doc[tor] was himself to have made the nomination of General Washington, but the state of the weather and of his health confined him to his house.[27]

Madison grasped the momentous nature of the convention more than most, conscientiously attending every session and taking copious notes. His written record of the proceedings, which would not be published until after his death in 1836, constitutes the most comprehensive documentation of the Constitutional Convention's historic debates and subsequent actions.

More state delegates arrived over the weekend, and the next session of the convention took place on Monday, May 28. It dealt primarily with establishing the various rules and the mundane procedures necessary to conduct orderly business. The members agreed that each of the states would have a single vote regardless of population or geographical size, mirroring the existing structure of the Confederation Congress under the Articles. Moreover, all of the convention's sessions were agreed to be conducted in private with the attending delegates sworn to secrecy in order to allow for an open and unfettered debate.[28] This self-imposed code of silence would effectively allow the various members the luxury of being able to express themselves freely and without fear of public censure. It had the additional benefit of providing them the autonomy to change their minds and alter their positions based upon persuasion or political necessity.

The Philadelphia Convention brought together the collective wisdom of some of the greatest political thinkers in the United States. They also brought with them their existing prejudices, personal self-interest, and human fallibility. Over the course of the ensuing three months, the representatives would argue, discuss, cajole, compromise, and complain. It remains one of the few times in human history that there was substantive and consequential debate concerning essential questions about governance and human freedom. What is the nature of government? How does a government maximize rights and liberty? What are the obligations and responsibilities of citizens? How is it possible to limit power and prevent tyranny?

After a tranquil beginning, the contentious debates began on May 29, when Virginia Governor Edmund Randolph first introduced the Virginia Plan.[29] The document had been conceived and written by James Madison and served to frame the course of subsequent discussions. Its fifteen resolutions called for a fundamental and radical alteration of the existing form of government and included provisions for the creation of a national two-house legislature. Madison insisted that state representation in this bicameral body be proportional, based upon the size of an individual state's population. Likewise, the Virginia Resolution called for the creation of a chief executive, the establishment of a national judiciary, and a systematic process of amendment.[30]

Objections to Virginia's proposal began almost immediately. Charles Pinckney of South Carolina wondered if the centralized system would abolish state governments.[31] Fellow South Carolinian, Edmund Rutledge, questioned whether the chief executive would have too much power, establishing a *de facto* monarchy in the United States.[32] But clearly the biggest obstacle to the plan came from the strong opposition of the small states, who demanded equality of representation in a national legislature. The delegates from these jurisdictions had just reason to be concerned. They feared that under the proposed system the small states would become irrelevant, at the mercy of the population titans—Virginia, Pennsylvania, and Massachusetts.[33] Luther Martin of Maryland dismissed the entire idea of proportional representation in Congress as little more than a "system of slavery."[34]

Further complicating the already tense situation was the insistence of southern delegates that slaves be included in any formula used for determining representation in the new Congress. This would, in effect, greatly inflate the region's influence in any national legislature, something that Gouverneur Morris of Pennsylvania exposed as preposterous.

> *Upon what principle is it that the slaves shall be computed in the representation? Are they men? Then make them Citizens and let them vote. Are they property? Why then is no other property included? The Houses in this city [Philadelphia] are worth more than all the wretched slaves which cover the rice swamps of South Carolina. The admission of slaves into the Representation when fairly explained comes to this: that the inhabitant of Georgia and S. C. who goes to the Coast of Africa, and in defiance of the most sacred laws of humanity tears away his fellow creatures from their dearest connections & damns them to the most cruel bondages, shall have more votes in a Govt instituted for protection of the rights of mankind, than the Citizen of Pa. or N. Jersey who views with a laudable horror, so nefarious a practice.[35]*

Despite significant opposition, ultimately a compromise was agreed to by which slaves would be counted as three-fifths of a person for purposes not only for representation but also for taxation.[36] This decision on slavery would have profound consequences for the nation and American history, but it would be deferred for future generations to solve.

On June 15, New Jersey responded and formally countered Virginia by introducing its own plan. Introduced by William Paterson, it called for the creation of a national, unicameral legislature with equal voting representation for all states, albeit with more power than that of the Confederation Congress.[37] James Madison argued effectively against what became known as the "small state" plan and was able to orchestrate its initial defeat by assembling a fragile coalition of southern and large states, but it was becoming obvious that the convention was rapidly teetering towards disaster. On July 16, when the time came for a final decision on the original proportional plan for the legislature, the vote was deadlocked. "So it was lost,"[38] a dismayed Madison wrote in his *Notes*. William Paterson quickly declared "that it was high time for the Convention to adjourn that the rule of secrecy ought to be rescinded and that our Constituents should be consulted."[39] There would be no concessions by the small states on the fundamental principle of equality.

Fortunately, cooler heads prevailed. Roger Sherman of Connecticut used the opportunity to reintroduce his previously rejected compromise proposal whereby the legislative branch would consist of a lower house—the House of Representatives—with representation based upon population and an upper house—the Senate—with the states equally represented. The motion miraculously passed by a single vote, pacifying both sides and saving the convention from dissolving into chaos.

As the new Constitution gradually began to take form, Madison's vision for an American republic became more apparent. Power under the federal system would be defused to prevent tyranny. Only the House of Representatives would be directly elected by the people and as such, it would be the more volatile assembly and subject to popular passions. The Senate would be appointed by the state legislatures with members serving six-year terms. Ideally, it would serve as the more deliberative and thoughtful body. As Madison explained, "The use of the Senate is to consist in its proceedings with more coolness, with more system, and with more wisdom, than the popular branch."[40] Finally, the executive would be chosen by electors appointed by the states and the judiciary appointed by the president and confirmed by the Senate. It was hoped by Madison that the government would thus be populated with the "purest and noblest characters" of American society.[41]

As the hot, miserable summer of 1787 drew to a close, the convention neared completion. A final version of the draft Constitution had been prepared and presented on September 12, when Elbridge Gerry and George Mason shocked the exhausted delegates by demanding the inclusion of a Bill of Rights. Mason claimed that this matter could be accomplished in a mere "few hours," but after weeks of agonizing debate, painful negotiation, and compromise, the other frustrated delegates disagreed. Besides, the Constitution as written had been carefully constructed with specific and clearly delineated powers; there was no need for a declaration of rights when these were already structurally secure. To add one would be dangerous since it would imply powers that the federal government clearly did not have. The vote against the proposal was unanimous, which further annoyed Gerry and Mason.[42]

Governor Edmund Randolph joined the two disgruntled delegates in their opposition to the final document. As the critical vote approached, Mason contentiously demanded that an entirely new convention be called and the entire process begun anew. "This Constitution had been formed without the knowledge or idea of the people," he said. "A second Convention will know more of the sense of the people, and be able to provide a system more consonant to it."[43] All such last-minute proposals were soundly defeated, and the Constitution was approved as written and ordered engrossed.

On Monday, September 17, 1787, the delegates gathered for the last time in the convention hall. After the Constitution was read to the assembly, an elderly Benjamin Franklin asked to be recognized. Realizing that some of the members still harbored ill-feelings, Franklin eloquently urged them to put aside their disagreements and support the new Constitution.

> *Mr. President*
>
> *I confess that there are several parts of this constitution which I do not at present approve, but I am not sure I shall never approve them: For having lived long, I have experienced many instances of being obliged by better information, or fuller consideration, to change opinions even on important subjects, which I once thought right, but found to be otherwise. It is therefore that the older I grow, the more apt I am to doubt my own judgment, and to pay more respect to the judgment of others ...*
>
> *From such an assembly can a perfect production be expected? It therefore astonishes me, Sir, to find this system approaching so near to perfection as it does; and I think it will astonish our enemies, who are waiting with confi-*

Virginia { *John Blair —*
James Madison Jr.

The Virginia Signers of the Constitution. James Madison and John Blair signed for Virginia, while George Washington signed as president of the Convention. George Mason and Edmund Randolph, however, refused to sign due to the document's failure to include an explicit Bill of Rights.

> *dence to hear that our councils are confounded like those of the Builders of Babel; and that our States are on the point of separation, only to meet hereafter for the purpose of cutting one another's throats. Thus I consent, Sir, to this Constitution because I expect no better, and because I am not sure, that it is not the best. The opinions I have had of its errors, I sacrifice to the public good. I have never whispered a syllable of them abroad. Within these walls they were born, and here they shall die …*
>
> *On the whole, Sir, I can not help expressing a wish that every member of the Convention who may still have objections to it, would with me, on this occasion doubt a little of his own infallibility, and to make manifest our unanimity, put his name to this instrument.[44]*

Despite his persuasive appeal for unanimity, Elbridge Gerry, George Mason, and Edmund Randolph still refused to sign the Constitution without the addition of a Bill of Rights. They would leave Philadelphia determined to orchestrate the Constitution's defeat during the forthcoming state ratification debates.[45] As James Madison noted in a letter to Thomas Jefferson, "Col. Mason left Philada. in an exceedingly ill humour indeed … He considers the want of a Bill of Rights as a fatal objection."[46]

George Washington, as the president of the convention, was the first member to sign the new Constitution. Ultimately thirty-nine men would attach their names to the historic document, including James Madison and John Blair from Virginia. Alexander Hamilton was the lone delegate from New York to sign, while Benjamin Franklin was one of eight signatories from Pennsylvania.[47] As he observed the other delegates signing the historic document, Franklin mused.

> *Looking towards the Presidents Chair, at the back of which a rising sun happened to be painted, observed to a few members near him, that Painters had*

found it difficult to distinguish in their art a rising from a setting sun. I have said he, often and often in the course of the Session, and the vicissitudes of my hopes and fears as to its issue, looked at that behind the President without being able to tell whether it was rising or setting: But now at length I have the happiness to know that it is a rising and not a setting Sun.[48]

With the business finally concluded, Madison ended his extensive notes by recording simply that "the Convention dissolved itself by Adjournment *sine die*."[49] There would, however, be no time for congratulations or celebration, since Article VII mandated that the states call special ratification conventions to approve the document. The magic number for approval was nine of the thirteen states, although the fate of the new government truly rested with the critical states of Massachusetts, Pennsylvania, New York, and Virginia.

Rather than return home to Virginia, James Madison instead travelled to New York to report to the Confederation Congress and to prepare for the ratification process. It proved to be a fortuitous decision, since opposition to the Constitution was already beginning to coalesce. The fragile nation's newspapers were filled with letters from its angry opponents, many making outlandish accusations and renewing demands that a new convention be convened.

Alexander Hamilton realized that the ultimate success and ratification of the document in his home state of New York was in serious jeopardy unless a reasoned and lucid response was rapidly organized. On October 27, 1787, writing under the pseudonym Publius, Hamilton published the first of what would become known as the *Federalist Papers*. These detailed explanations of the philosophy and structure of the Constitution were intended for the "People of the State of New York," but the articles were circulated and republished in several news-

George Washington's chair from the Constitutional Convention. Benjamin Franklin observed that the ornamentation on the chair was a rising sun, symbolic of the political birth of the new republic.

papers throughout the United States, thus expanding their political impact.[50] In just three weeks, Hamilton prolifically published seven of his sophisticated political essays and was successfully able to enlist Madison's help in contributing to this vital political endeavor.[51] Madison's first essay, "The Federalist No. 10," appeared in the newspapers on November 21.[52]

Since the veil of secrecy had finally been lifted from the delegates, Madison felt that it was his duty to inform Thomas Jefferson about the Convention's outcome, fully aware that his old friend may well oppose in theory the final document. In a long and extended seventeen-page letter, Madison attempted to reassure Jefferson that the Convention had been nothing "less than a miracle."[53] Its political remedy was desperately needed, but Jefferson, having lived abroad for four years and isolated from the domestic turmoil, failed to fully grasp the continuing damage being done to the nation by the want of effective government. Although Jefferson was a great theorist and brilliant thinker, he regularly failed to appreciate the stark realities of the political world or the darker side of human nature. Madison would later excuse these notable lapses by explaining that "allowances ought to be made for a Habit in Mr. Jefferson as in others of great Genius in expressing in strong and round Terms, impressions of the moment."[54]

As expected, Jefferson's response to the new Constitution was tepid. His return letter to Madison listed his extensive objections along with the caveat, "I am not a friend to a very energetic government. It is always oppressive."[55] He also sided with the cantankerous George Mason on the need for the inclusion of a Bill of Rights. "A bill of rights is what the people are entitled to against every government on earth, general or particular, and what no just government should refuse, or rest on inference."[56] He ended his discourse by expressing his preference for the will of the majority.

> *After all, it is my principle that the will of the Majority should always prevail. If they approve the proposed Convention in all it's [sic] parts, I shall concur in it cheerfully, in hopes that they will amend it whenever they shall find it work wrong. I think our governments will remain virtuous for many centuries; as long as they are chiefly agricultural; and this will be as long as there shall be vacant lands in any part of America. When they get piled upon one another in large cities, as in Europe, they will become corrupt as in Europe. Above all things I hope the education of the common people will be attended to; convinced*

that on their good sense we may rely with the most security for the preservation
of a due degree of liberty.[57]

Over the next several months, Jefferson's considerable musings would often be used by the anti-federalist opponents of the Constitution to justify their positions. Still, Madison continued to carefully and methodically explain the principles of the new, republican government in his ongoing contributions to the *Federalist Papers*. In "The Federalist No. 49," he explained that the proposed government would have an elaborate system of checks and balances that would help prevent abuse. Furthermore, by structurally dividing power between the three branches of government, this would help thwart tyrannical impulses. Madison recognized the absolute necessity of creating a government of limited and defined powers to ameliorate the effects of the public's propensity to promote its self interests over the nation's general welfare. In an ideal world, Madison wrote, reasoned judgment along with a "reverence for the laws would be sufficiently inculcated by the voice of an enlightened reason." This was sheer fantasy since "a nation of philosophers is as little to be expected as the philosophical race of kings wished for by Plato."[58] His most famous essay, "The Federalist No. 51," went even further.

> *But what is government itself, but the greatest of all reflections on human nature? If men were angels, no government would be necessary. If angels were to govern men, neither external nor internal controls on government would be necessary. In framing a government which is to be administered by men over men, the great difficulty lies in this: you must first enable the government to control the governed; and in the next place oblige it to control itself.*[59]

Several of the state ratifying conventions had already met by early spring 1788 and the Constitution had passed easily in all but Massachusetts, where the vote was a razor-thin 187-168 in favor.[60] The true test of the document, though, would come in Virginia and New York, where there was considerable opposition, and the ratifying conventions would not meet until June.

The Virginia Convention assembled in Richmond on June 2, 1788. James Madison had been elected as a delegate from Orange County, while both Patrick Henry and George Mason had been selected to represent their constituencies. Edmund Pendleton was voted to serve as the chairman.[61]

The delegates agreed that they would discuss the Constitution clause by clause, a tactic that clearly favored Madison and his encyclopedic knowledge of the document.[62] But it was Patrick Henry who fired the opening salvo of the debate with his typically compelling oratory. He challenged the very legitimacy of the Constitution Convention, contending that it was an insidious effort aimed at destroying the existing states.

> *Have they said, We, the states? Have they made a proposal of a compact between states? If they had, this would be a confederation. It is otherwise most clearly a consolidated government. The question turns, sir, on that poor little thing—the expression. We, the people, instead of the states, of America. I need not take much pains to show that the principles of this system are extremely pernicious, impolitic, and dangerous. . . . Here is a resolution as radical as that which separated us from Great Britain. It is radical in this transition; our rights and privileges are endangered, and the sovereignty of the states will be relinquished.[63]*

Ignoring the decision of the convention to deal with the specifics of the document, Henry continued to use generalities and assertions to question the principles and philosophy of the new government. He demanded that substantive, structural amendments be added to the original document, but alleged that if the new Constitution were adopted, it precluded the states from asserting their power to do so.

> *The necessity of amendments is universally admitted. I ask, if amendments be necessary, from whence can they be so properly proposed as from this state? The example of Virginia is a powerful thing, particularly with respect to North Carolina, whose supplies must come through Virginia. Every possible opportunity of procuring amendments is gone, our power and political salvation are gone, if we ratify unconditionally.[64]*

Madison stoically endured Henry's tirades until it was finally his time to respond. He knew that to effectively counter Henry's eloquence, Madison would have to persuade the Virginia delegates with logic and facts. He urged the members of the convention to avoid being emotionally swayed by oratory and rhetoric and instead

> *examine the Constitution on its own merits solely: we are to inquire whether it will promote the public happiness: its aptitude to produce this desirable object ought to be the exclusive subject of our present researches. In this pursuit, we ought not to address our arguments to the feelings and passions, but to those*

understandings and judgments which were selected by the people of this country,
to decide this great question by a calm and rational investigation.[65]

Over the next several days of heated debate, Madison spoke regularly, some-times delivering as many as seven speeches in a single day. John Marshall later observed that "Mr. Henry had without the greatest power to persuade. Mr. Madi-son had the greatest power to convince."[66]

It had been a strategic decision not to allow the ratification conventions to alter the Constitution. The document would have to be either accepted or rejected as a whole to ensure that all of the states were considering the same document. As Alexander Hamilton later wrote, "The Constitution requires an adoption *in toto*, and *for ever.*"[67] Madison was forced to concede that the first Congress would consider amendments, but this would only occur after the gov-ernment had been approved and was functional. The Henry faction was livid and unwilling to trust the good intentions of the Constitution's supporters. Henry again questioned, "Do you enter into a compact first, and afterwards settle the terms of the government?"[68]

After three weeks of heated discussions, the final vote on ratification in Vir-ginia was eighty-nine in favor with seventy-nine opposed. George Wythe's com-mittee added a caveat to the approval, expressing the delegates' expectation that the new Congress should add a bill of rights, and provided a list of suggested amendments.

New Hampshire had become the ninth state to ratify the Constitution a few days earlier, which technically fulfilled the requirement for the new document to go into effect, but the Virginia decision was far more important. It had a direct influence on the outcome of the vote in New York, where the document passed the following month by a slim thirty to twenty-seven vote in favor. Although North Carolina and Rhode Island would not ratify until later, and hence would not participate in the first federal elections, the remaining ratifying states began preparations for the meeting of the new government in 1789.

Madison once again returned to New York and wrote to Thomas Jefferson about the final positive outcome of the ratification debates. Jefferson responded graciously, but again gently reminded Madison of the need for the inclusion of a Bill of Rights. "I sincerely rejoice at the acceptance of our new constitution by nine states. It is a good canvas, on which some strokes only want retouching."[69]

Madison responded to Jefferson's letter by outlining his hopes that a pre-dominantly federalist government would soon be elected and which would be

NATIONAL ARCHIVES

The Preamble from the United States Constitution. The phrase "We the People" indicated the founders' belief that the document derived its sovereignty from the nation's citizens rather than from the state governments.

committed to the implementation of the new federal Constitution. Madison himself would be elected to the first House of Representatives, and George Washington's election as the nation's first president was a foregone conclusion, Madison explained.

> *Notwithstanding the formidable opposition made to the new federal government, first in order to prevent its adoption, and since in order to place its administration in the hands of disaffected men, there is now both a certainty of its peaceable commencement in March next, and a flattering prospect that it will be administ[ered] by men who will give it a fair trial. General Washington will certainly be called to the Executive department. Mr. Adams who is pledged to support him will probably be the vice president.* [70]

The successful ratification of the U.S. Constitution was, in many ways, the final chapter of the American Revolution. The new republican structure provided a remarkably practical and stable government that guaranteed the theoretical rights that had ostensibly been won on the battlefield. Near the end of his life, Madison would marvel, "The happy union of these States is a wonder: their Constitution a miracle: their example the hope of Liberty throughout the World."[71]

ENDNOTES

Epigraph: Adrienne Koch quoted in William Lee Miller, *The Business of Next May: James Madison and the Founding* (Charlottesville: University of Virginia Press, 1992), 15.

[1] Elbridge Gerry quoted in Leonard L. Richards, *Shay's Rebellion: The American Revolution's Final Battle* (Philadelphia: University of Pennsylvania Press, 2002),, 134.

[2] Light Horse Harry Lee to James Madison, October 25, 1786, in R.A. Rutland, *The Papers of James Madison: 9 April 1786-24 May 1787,* (Chicago: University of Chicago Press, 1975), 145.

[3] Madison in Rutland, *Papers of James Madison: 10 March 1784-28 March 1786,* 278.

[4] Thomas Jefferson quoted in Peterson, 102.

[5] Thomas Jefferson to James Madison, December 20, 1787 in James Morton Smith, 514.

[6] Thomas Jefferson to William Stephens Smith, November 13, 1787, in Bernard Bailyn, ed., *The Debate on the Constitution: Federalists and Antifederalist Speeches during the Struggle over Ratification* (New York: Library of America, 1993), 310.

[7] Under the provisions of the Articles, each state had one vote in the national legislature but could send

a delegation consisting of between two and seven delegates.

[8] Ketcham, *James Madison: A Biography,* 185.

[9] Madison's notes on "Ancient and Modern Confederacies" are reprinted in their entirety in Robert A. Rutland, ed., *The Papers of James Madison: 9 April 1786-24 May 1787* (Chicago: University of Chicago Press, 1975), 4-24.

[10] Rutland, *9 April 1786-24 May 1787,* p. 4.

[11] Madison, "Vices of the Political System of the United States," quoted in Rutland, *9 April 1786-24 May 1787,* 350.

[12] Ibid., 350.

[13] Ibid., 351-352.

[14] Ibid., 353.

[15] Ibid., 353.

[16] Ibid., 357.

[17] Ibid., 422.

[18] William Lee Miller, *Business of Next May,* 61. The entire six-member Virginia delegation comprised John Blair, James Madison, James McClurg, George Mason, George Washington, and George Wythe.

[19] Washington was known as an American "Cincinnatus." In 457 BC, Lucius Quinctius Cincinnatus was called out of retirement to save Rome from an enemy tribe. He left his farm to take up the sword in the defense of his country. Once the enemy was defeated, Cincinnatus willingly gave up power and returned to his farm rather than become the permanent dictator of Rome. The analogy of Washington and his service in the American Revolution was apropos.

[20] Madison to Thomas Jefferson, May 15, 1787, quoted in Rutland, *9 April 1786-24 May 1787,* 415.

[21] Mayer, *Son of Thunder,* 370.

[22] Madison to George Washington, March 18, 1787, quoted in Rutland, *9 April 1786-24 May 1787,* 316.

[23] It would be decided in a subsequent session that a quorum would consist of seven states.

[24] David O. Stewart, *The Summer of 1787: The Men Who Invented the Constitution* (New York: Simon & Schuster, 2007), 47.

[25] See James Madison's notes on the Constitutional Convention republished in a modern edition by Adrienne Koch, *Notes of Debates in the Federal Convention of 1787 Reported by James Madison,* (Athens: Ohio University Press, 1984), 23.

[26] Madison quoted in Stewart, 48.

[27] Madison, *Notes,* 24.

[28] Ibid., 24-27.

[29] Bailyn, 1047-1048.

[30] Ibid., 30-33. The actual document (the Virginia Plan) can be viewed at the National Archives in Washington, D.C. It is available digitally at: http://www.archives.gov/historical-docs/

[31] Ibid., 34.

[32] Ibid., 67.

[33] Ibid., 95.

[34] Luther Martin quoted in Stewart, 102.

[35] Gouverneur Morris quoted in Madison, 411.

[36] See Article I, Section 2 of the United States Constitution.

[37] Madison, *Notes,* 117.

[38] Ibid., 299.

[39] William Paterson quoted in Madison, 299.

[40] Madison, *Notes,* 83.

[41] See The Federalist No. 10.

[42] Madison, *Notes,* 630.

[43] Ibid., 651.

[44] Franklin's speech to the Convention quoted by Madison, *Notes,* 653- 654.

[45] Stewart, 240.

[46] Madison to Thomas Jefferson, October 24, 1787, quoted in Bailyn, p. 203.

[47] New Hampshire had two signatories; Massachusetts–two; Connecticut–two; New York–one; New Jersey–four; Pennsylvania–eight; Delaware–five; Maryland–three; Virginia–three including George Wash-

ington; North Carolina–three; South Carolina–four; and Georgia–two. Rhode Island would not ratify the Constitution until 1790.

[48] Franklin quoted by Madison, *Notes*, 659.

[49] Madison, *Notes,* 659.

[50] Syrett and Cooke, *Papers of Alexander Hamilton,* 287-288.

[51] John Jay also contributed to *The Federalist Papers.* According to historian Adrienne Koch, "Jay's contribution of eight numbers, none of them first-rate, hardly justifies giving him a full share in the collaboration." Koch, *Jefferson and Madison: The Great Collaboration,* 48. The authorship of some of the papers remains in doubt. Most historians credit Madison with writing twenty-nine essays, Hamilton fifty-one, and Jay five. Ketcham, *James Madison: A Biography,* 239.

[52] Ketcham, *James Madison: A Biography* , 239.

[53] Madison quoted in James Morton Smith, 446.

[54] Madison to James Robertson, April 20, 1831, available at: http://www.jmu.edu/madison/center/main_pages/madison_archives/quotes/great/constitution.htm.

[55] Thomas Jefferson quoted in James Morton Smith, 450.

[56] Jefferson quoted in James Morton Smith, 451.

[57] Thomas Jefferson to James Madison, December 20, 1787, in James Morton Smith, 514.

[58] *The Federalist Papers* are readily available online from a variety of sources including the Avalon Project at the Yale Law School. See The Federalist No. 49 available at: http://www.yale.edu/lawweb/avalon/federal/fed.htm.

[59] The Federalist No. 51.

[60] In December 1788, Delaware, Pennsylvania, and New Jersey had ratified the Constitution. Georgia and Connecticut approved the document in January, followed by Massachusetts in February. By the time the Virginia, New York, and New Hampshire conventions began in June, eight states had approved the document.

[61] Ketchum, 253.

[62] Ibid., 254.

[63] Patrick Henry quoted in Richard D. Brown, *Major Problems in the Era of the American Revolution: 1760-1791*, Major Problems in American History. New York, Houghton-Mifflin Company, 2000), 456.

[64] Henry quoted in Brown, 457.

[65] Madison quoted in Peterson, 157.

[66] John Marshall quoted in Joseph Ellis, *American Creation: Triumphs and Tragedies at the Founding of the Republic* (New York: Alfred A. Knopf, 2007), 121.

[67] James Madison quoted in Robert Morton Smith, 521.

[68] Patrick Henry quoted in Peterson, 161.

[69] Thomas Jefferson to James Madison, July 31, 1788, in Robert Morton Smith, 545.

[70] James Madison to Thomas Jefferson, December 8, 1788, in Robert Morton Smith, 579.

[71] David B. Mattern, ed., *James Madison's "Advice to My Country."* Charlottesville, University Press of Virginia, 1997).

CHAPTER FIVE

Rights, Sedition, and War

The name of Madison, celebrated in America, is well known in Europe by
the merited eulogium made of him by his countryman and friend Mr. Jefferson.
Though still young he has rendered the greatest services to Virginia,
to the American Confederation, and to liberty and humanity in general ...
His look announces a censor, his conversation discovers the man of learning,
and his reserve was that of a man conscious of his talents and of his duties.
— J.P. BRISSOT DE WARVILLE

T he Confederation Congress of the United States of America quietly expired on October 10, 1788, unmourned and unlamented. In one of its final acts, the legislature set the time for the convening of the new Constitutional government, which the states were scheduled to elect over the ensuing few months. James Madison spent his final days as a Virginia representative by continuing to fend off renewed calls for a second Constitutional Convention. This only served to increase Madison's apprehensions about the growing mobilization of anti-federal sentiment in the various state legislatures. Despite the successful ratification of the Constitution, the Anti-Federalists still posed a serious threat to the ultimate fate of the country; if they were successful in their efforts to gain political control of the nation's Senate and House of Representatives, the new Constitution would be in jeopardy. At a minimum, they would propose dangerous, structural amendments that would disrupt the delicate balance of power that had been miraculously achieved in Philadelphia. At worse, they would cripple the new government by stripping it of its power and making it as impotent as its predecessor.

With North Carolina and Rhode Island still obstinately refusing to ratify the Constitution as written and thus ineligible to participate in the upcoming federal elections, the danger of political disunion was painfully apparent to Madison. The news from Virginia was equally ominous, since Patrick Henry remained angry and embittered over his strategic defeat at the state's ratification convention. The undeterred Henry continued to promote an openly anti-constitutional agenda. George Washington remarked on Henry's legendary political power within the state legislature.

> The whole proceedings of the Assembly, it is said may be summed up in one word—to wit—that the Edicts of Mr H[enry] are enregistered with less opposition by the Majority of that body, than those of the Grand Monarch are in the Parliaments of France. He has only to say let this be Law—and it is Law.[1]

Edward Carrington likewise alerted Madison of the dangers within the Virginia state legislature. "I am confident that two thirds of the Assembly are Anti's who meditate mischief against the Govt."[2]

Under the original provisions of Article I of the new Constitution, the individual legislatures were empowered to appoint their state's two allotted senators. Although Henry personally refused to seek the office for himself, he actively advanced the candidacies of two avowed "antis," Richard Henry Lee and William Grayson.[3] Madison was likewise nominated by the pro-federal faction in the Richmond legislature but Henry denounced the choice, claiming that Madison would not advance Virginia's cause in Congress, nor would he propose the much needed amendments to rectify the Constitution's "many" deficiencies. Henry launched a vindictive and exaggerated personal attack against Madison, which Richard Henry Lee later confided to him. "[Henry] exclaimed against your political character, and pronounced you unworthy of the confidence of the people in the station of senator. That your election would terminate in producing rivulets of blood throughout the land."[4]

Henry was ultimately successful in his manipulations to secure the Senate seats for both Lee and Grayson, but his vile tactics prompted disgust and prophesizing from one

LIBRARY OF CONGRESS

Patrick Henry of Virginia. Henry was a vocal opponent of the Constitution and maneuvered to block James Madison's appointment by the state legislature to the Senate. Likewise, he tried unsuccessfully to deny Madison's election to the first House of Representatives.

delegate who witnessed the process. "Hereafter, when a gentleman is nominated to a public office, it is not his virtue, his abilities, or his patriotism we are to regard, but whether he is a federalist or an antifederalist."[5]

Madison's only hope now for participating in the opening session of the new legislature was to stand for popular election to the House of Representatives. This would require Madison to return to Virginia to actively campaign and solicit votes from his neighbors and constituents. As he penned to George Washington, it was something that he was loathed to do. "I have an extreme distaste to steps having an electioneering appearance."[6]

Compounding Madison's dilemma was the fact that Patrick Henry, his political nemesis, had cleverly "gerrymandered" Madison's congressional district to maximize the region's anti-federal sentiment.[7] Spanning almost 80 miles and stretching from Fredericksburg to the Blue Ridge Mountains, it comprised eight huge Virginia counties. For the always physically frail James Madison, to actively campaign for office over such large distances in the dead of winter would prove both physically and logistically challenging.[8]

Madison finally returned home to Virginia in December 1788, stopping en route at Mount Vernon to consult with General Washington. Madison's opponent for his district's House seat was the formidable James Monroe. Monroe was a distinguished Revolutionary War hero, a prominent politician, and an acknowledged Anti-federalist; but notwithstanding their considerable political differences, Madison and Monroe knew and respected each other.[9] They eventually agreed to campaign together throughout the massive Fifth Congressional district and would jointly appear before gatherings of interested citizens to argue the merits and flaws of the new Constitution. Both men were conspicuously careful not to impugn the other's character, and the resulting political debate was truly a substantive political discussion free from the vengeful personal attacks and demagoguery that would characterize later political campaigns. "Between ourselves," Madison recalled, "I have no reason to doubt that the distinction was duly kept in mind between political and personal views, and it has saved our friendship from the smallest diminution."[10]

It became obvious to Madison that his district's voters were strongly in favor of the inclusion of a Bill of Rights in the new Constitution. He had slowly come to accept this as inevitable and was willing to consider a few carefully crafted amendments that explicitly guaranteed individual liberties to gain popular support for the new government. "Amendments," Madison wrote, "if pursued with a proper moderation and in a proper mode, will be not only safe, but may serve the double purpose of satisfying the minds of well meaning opponents, and of providing additional guards in favour of liberty."[11] As such, Madison solemnly pledged to his constituents that, if elected, he would personally introduce such legislation during the first session of Congress.

The actual voting for the House of Representatives took place in Virginia on a brutally cold and snowy February 2, 1789. All eligible voters were, at that time, required by law to cast their ballots personally at the local courthouse. Despite the inhospitable conditions, the turnout was remarkable and the result fateful, with Madison defeating James Monroe by a solid 326-vote plurality. According to author Richard Labunski, this was the single most important Congressional election in American history, since it ensured James Madison's presence in the first Congress, where he would help maintain a fidelity to the new Constitution while strategically preventing the opposition from subverting the new government.[12]

The First Congress of the United States began to assemble as scheduled in New York on March 4, 1789, but with the usual lack of legislative urgency, it took an additional three weeks before the House and Senate achieved the necessary quorum. The most pressing order of business was to tally the electoral votes for president that had been submitted from the eleven participating states. As expected, George Washington was unanimously elected, while John Adams was chosen to serve as vice president.[13]

As the Congress anxiously awaited the arrival of General Washington in New York for his inauguration, little else of substance was accomplished. The cantankerous William Maclay, senator from Pennsylvania, impatiently noted in his journal, "Ceremonies endless ceremonies the whole business of the day."[14] Madison more thoughtfully considered the incredible obstacles facing the successful implementation of a new republican government. He wrote to Thomas Jefferson that there were no established precedents to consult. "We are in a wilderness without a single footstep to guide us,"[15] he said.

George Washington's journey from Mount Vernon to New York was a prolonged, triumphal celebration of the new American republic. Each city along his route staged elaborate welcoming ceremonies for the great hero of the American Revolution. In New Jersey, Washington was greeted by a select congressional delegation; together they boarded a specially commissioned barge to sail up the Hudson River to the provisional capital of the United States.

Washington arrived in New York City with great fanfare on April 23, a full week before his scheduled inauguration, giving him ample time to prepare for the important ceremonies.[16] He had asked James Madison to review a draft of his intended 73-page speech to Congress, which Madison politely and delicately informed him was far too long and inappropriate for the occasion. Heeding the advice, a much more modest and consolidated draft emphasizing general republican principles was soon completed.[17]

At precisely 1 p.m. on April 30, George Washington stood stoically on the balcony of Federal Hall as the solemn oath of office was administered. The multitude of citizens who gathered to witness the historic event, shouted their approval of the new president before he retired to the Senate Chamber to deliver his now abbreviated inaugural address. There he urged the assembled representatives to consider seriously their considerable responsibilities under Article V (the process for amending the Constitution) and to "carefully avoid every alteration which might endanger the benefits of a United and effective government."[18] The government of the United States of America was now functioning under the provisions dictated by the Constitution.

Six states, including Virginia, had already sent extensive lists of suggested amendments that they wished to be considered by the Congress.[19] Many over-

George Washington's Inaugural Address painted by T.H. Matteson. George Washington was inaugurated as the nation's first president on April 30, 1789. Madison helped edit the president's inaugural address, which was delivered in the Senate Chamber. The speech urged the new Congress to use judgment and wisdom when proposing amendments to the Constitution.

Federal Hall in New York City. The new government convened at Federal Hall in 1789. It took several weeks before the House and Senate were able to achieve a quorum. North Carolina and Rhode Island did not participate, having failed to ratify the Constitution.

lapped and involved specific guarantees of individual rights. There were some proposals of more questionable intent and even a few that were intentionally designed to sabotage the basic structure of the government.

Madison was resolute in his efforts to seize the initiative and to gain control over the amendment process. He was also determined to honor and fulfill his solemn campaign pledge to his constituents to introduce specific amendments for a Bill of Rights to be incorporated into the Constitution. He informed the delegates in the House of Representatives of his intent to compile a list of changes that would emphasize the rights of citizens as well as provide explicit guarantees of liberty.

On June 8, 1789, Madison rose to address the House chamber. "I considered myself bound in honor and in duty to do what I have done on this subject," he explained, "[and] I shall proceed to bring the amendments before you as soon as possible, and advocate them until they shall be finally adopted or rejected by a Constitutional majority of this House."[20] Several congressmen directly objected to Madison's proposal, insisting that it was far too premature. The Congress had been in session for only a few weeks and was still in the process of developing its proper parliamentary procedures and struggling to find its legislative character. Representative James Jackson of Georgia in exasperation commented, "Let the Constitution have a fair trial; let it be examined by experience, discover by that test what its errors are, and then talk of amending; but to attempt it now is doing it at a risk, which is certainly imprudent."[21]

Madison calmly countered each objection by explaining the necessity of pacifying the many well-meaning opponents of the current Constitution.

> It will be a desirable thing to extinguish from the bosom of every member of the community, any apprehensions that there are those among his countrymen who wish to deprive them of the liberty for which they valiantly fought and honorably bled. And if there are amendments desired of such a nature as will not injure the Constitution, and they can be ingrafted so as to give satisfaction to the doubting part of our fellow-citizens, the friends of the Federal Government will evince that spirit of deference and concession for which they have hitherto been distinguished ... If I thought I could fulfil the duty which I owe to myself and my constituents, to let the subject pass over in silence, I most certainly should not trespass upon the indulgence of this House. But I cannot do this, and am therefore compelled to beg a patient hearing to what I have to lay before you ... there is a great number of our constituents who are dissatisfied with it; among whom are many respectable for their talents and patriotism, and respectable for the jealousy they have for their liberty, which, though mistaken in its object, is laudable in its motive.[22]

He then offered several revisions, which he had culled from the various proposals submitted by the states, to refine and reassert republican principles. These proposals were relegated to a congressional committee that would consider, debate, and revise them. The process was protracted and took several weeks of deliberation before seventeen amendments were finally reported out of the committee and adopted by the House of Representatives as a whole. After these proposals were sent to the Senate for consideration, they were consolidated and reduced to twelve amendments, which were then sent on to the states for ratification under the provisions outlined in Article V.[23]

Madison adamantly believed that any and all subsequent amendments to the United States Constitution be incorporated into the actual text of the document, inserted at the appropriate place rather than attached as a codicil. This, he felt, would preclude the danger of creating a separate and rival document that some opponents could use to weaken the original Constitution.[24] Roger Sherman of Connecticut, however, argued persuasively that the primary wording of the Constitution had to remain completely intact, unaltered, and pristine, while amendments should be added separately to the end of the document, albeit superseding the original text. His logic was sound, based upon the fact that the Constitution had been ratified by special conventions elected by the people, while the amendments were essentially a decision of the Congress in conjunction with the individual state legislatures.

> *We ought not to interweave our propositions into the work itself, because it will be destructive of the whole fabric. We might as well endeavor to mix brass, iron, and clay, as to incorporate such heterogeneous articles; the one contradictory to the other … When an alteration is made in an act, it is done by way of supplement … The constitution is the act of the people, and ought to remain entire. It was a powerful line of reasoning and one that eventually prevailed.[25]*

Over the course of the next two years, each of the state legislatures considered the proposed amendments to the Constitution. North Carolina, finally mollified, ratified both the Constitution and approved the Bill of Rights in short order. Rhode Island remained obstinate but finally did likewise by the narrowest of majorities—thirty-four to thirty-two. On December 15, 1791, the Virginia legislature ratified ten of the proposed amendments, achieving the three-fourths majority necessary for adoption.[26] The Bill of Rights now joined the Constitution and the Declaration of Independence, completing the triad comprising the nation's founding documents. James Madison had played a critical role in the adoption of two of these important charters of freedom.

Throughout the two terms of George Washington's presidential administration, foreign intrigue continued to intrude upon the nation's domestic priorities and the country's ongoing quest to secure a national identity. Britain and France, habitually at war, were recklessly violating American neutrality and shipping rights, scorning the nation's independence and sovereignty. At the same time, internal political divisions within the United States intensified over substantive philosophical and governmental differences that directly led to the development of two distinct parties. The "Federalists" were heavily concentrated in the New England region and consisted primarily of merchants, tradesmen, and infant capitalists. Championed by Secretary of the Treasury Alexander Hamilton and Vice President John Adams, the Federalist Party favored a strong central government, sound fiscal principles, and a pro-British foreign policy. Opposing them were the so-called "Democratic-Republicans." They were led unofficially by Secretary of State Thomas Jefferson and Congressman James Madison. The Democratic-Republicans favored a renewed commitment to sacred republican principles, strict interpretation of the Constitution, agrarian self-sufficiency, and a pro-French foreign policy. Madison elaborated on the substantive political differences between the two parties in a candid but biased account published in Philip Freneau's *National Gazette* in 1792.

> *[The Federalists] are more partial to the opulent than to the other classes of society; and having debauched themselves into a persuasion that mankind are incapable of governing themselves, it follows with them, of course, that government can be carried on only by the pageantry of rank, the influence of money and emoluments, and the terror of military force ... [The Democratic-Republicans] consists of those who believing in the doctrine that mankind are capable of governing themselves, and hating hereditary power as an insult to the reason and an outrage to the rights of man, are naturally offended at every public measure that does not appeal to the understanding and to the general interest of the community, or that is not strictly conformable to the principles, and conducive to the preservation of republican government.[27]*

For the Democratic-Republicans, the French Revolution was viewed as an imperfect mirror of the American Revolution and a logical expansion of republican ideals. Yet, despite the extraordinary domestic upheaval in France where the blood of king, noble, priest, and dissident flowed freely, Thomas Jefferson was once again willing to excuse the excesses. As he expressed in a remarkable letter written in 1793, he hoped that the ultimate advancement and triumph of liberty would justify the sacrifice.

> *The liberty of the whole earth was depending on the issue of the contest, and was ever such a prize won with so little innocent blood? My own affections have been deeply wounded by some of the martyrs to this cause, but rather than it should have failed, I would have seen half the earth desolated. Were there but an Adam & an Eve left in every country, & left free, it would be better than as it now is.[28]*

Federalist John Adams saw things more sensibly, stating "that there was not a single principle the same in the American and French Revolutions."[29]

The party divisions continued to escalate. In 1796, the Senate narrowly ratified the controversial Jay's Treaty, making the political rift irreparable. The treaty was seen as a triumph for the Federalists, effectively averting the immediate potential of war with the British by reaffirming the two nations' historical trade relationship. But it also served to outrage the French who saw the agreement as a de facto economic alliance between the their sworn enemy and the United States. The Democratic-Republicans, along with James Madison, opposed the pact, calling it a "ruinous bargain."[30]

Jay's Treaty was, in effect, the last major political act of Washington's presidency. The General was determined not to seek a third term, and his impending retirement set the stage for the first truly contested presidential election in American history. Washington was troubled by the increasing animosity and acrimony between the two partisan political factions, and he used his Farewell Address to Congress to warn about the dangers of such internal political divisions.

> *I have already intimated to you the danger of parties in the State ... [Let me also] warn you in the most solemn manner against the baneful effects of the spirit of party generally. This spirit, unfortunately, is inseparable from our nature, having its root in the strongest passions of the human mind ... The alternate domination of one faction over another, sharpened by the spirit of revenge, natural to party dissension, which in different ages and countries has perpetrated the most horrid enormities, is itself a frightful despotism ... It serves always to distract the public councils and enfeeble the public administration. It agitates the community with ill-founded jealousies and false alarms, kindles the animosity of one part against another, foments occasionally riot and insurrection. It opens the door to foreign influence and corruption, which finds a facilitated access to the government itself through the channels of party passions. Thus the policy and the will of one country are subjected to the policy and will of another.[31]*

The Federalists selected Vice President John Adams as their candidate for president. Opposing him was the Democratic-Republican nominee, Thomas Jefferson. But unlike modern presidential elections, neither candidate actively or overtly campaigned for office, since there was no popular vote for president. Instead each of the sixteen individual state legislatures was empowered by the Constitution to select committed electors who would then cast their individual votes for president.[32] Thus it was the political makeup of the individual state houses that was critical for election.[33]

Despite some political intrigue covertly waged by Alexander Hamilton, John Adams ultimately carried nine states by assembling a delicate coalition of the New England and Mid-Atlantic regions. Jefferson carried seven states, including the entire South, along with the Commonwealth of Pennsylvania. In the Electoral College, Adams received the necessary absolute majority to win the presidency, but his plurality was a razor thin three electoral votes—seventy-one to sixty-eight. According to the provisions of the Constitution at that time, the candidate who received the second-highest number of votes for president, regardless of political affiliation, became vice president. Thus, despite his considerable political differences with Adams, Thomas Jefferson was elected to service in this capacity. He claimed, perhaps somewhat pretentiously, that he was content with the outcome. "The second office [the Vice Presidency]," he wrote, "is honorable and easy, the first is but splendid misery."[34]

NATIONAL ARCHIVES

President John Adams. During John Adams's presidency, the rift between the Federal and Democratic-Republican parties increased. Although James Madison had hoped to retire from public office, the passage of the hated Alien and Sedition Acts led him back into public service.

The new president, in a rare spirit of bipartisanship, offered James Madison an appointment to serve as an American minister to France, but Madison rejected the offer. Having seen the Constitution successfully implemented over the first decisive years of the republic, he was anxious to retire from elective office and was anticipating returning to Montpelier with his new wife, Dolley, and his stepson, Payne. In a letter to his father, Madison asked that his desire to withdraw from public life be honored and that all efforts be made to ensure that he was not elected to the Virginia state legislature in absentia. "I repeat my request that my name may not be suffered to get on the Poll for the County election ... In declining to go into the Assembly, should there really be a disposition to send me there I am sincere & inflexible."[35] A politically astute John Adams questioned Madison's true intentions in a letter to Abigail. "It seems the Mode of becoming great is to retire. Madison I suppose after a Retirement of a few Years is to become President or V. P. It is marvelous how political Plants grow in the shade" [36]

Whatever fanciful hopes Adams may have had initially for a reduction of political tensions quickly evaporated as French naval vessels continued to prey upon American merchant vessels. Compounding the international situation was Napoleon Bonaparte's military adventurism and his triumphal campaigns.

These events had little direct impact upon the Virginia piedmont and, by January 1798, Madison was absorbed by his long planned renovations at Montpelier. He was enjoying the respite from the bitter partisan politics of the era, but his domestic tranquility was short-lived. In Congress, tensions between the Federalists and the Democratic-Republicans remained at an all-time high. One representative, Matthew Lyon (Democratic-Republican) of Vermont, took umbrage at a personal slur made against him during a speech delivered by fellow member Roger Griswold (Federalist) of Connecticut. Breaking all parliamentary decorum, Lyon angrily crossed the aisle, confronted Griswold, and spit into his face, thereby forever earning the epithet, The Spitting Lyon. In many ways, the lamentable incident symbolized the deterioration of all civility and decorum within the government. Two weeks later, Griswold retaliated unexpectedly by cane-whipping Lyon during a session of the House of Representatives. The ensuing fight and pathetic spectacle reduced Congress to what one representative referred to as "an assembly of Gladiators."[37] James Madison, writing to Vice President Jefferson, noted, "The affair of

"Congressional Pugilists." Political tensions erupted into violence on the floor of the House of Representatives when Representative Roger Griswold attacked and cane-whipped fellow delegate, Matthew Lyon. One astute observer lamented that the Congress had degenerated into "an assembly of Gladiators."

Lyon & Griswold is bad eno' every way; but worst of all in becoming a topic of tedious & disgraceful debates in Congress."[38] The Lyon-Griswold spectacle, lampooned in a famous print titled "Congressional Pugilist," was an aberration where two individuals allowed consequential disagreements to degenerate into personal slurs and physical retaliation. It was an embarrassment to both political parties.

French outrages against American shipping in international waters continued unabated, but, to his credit, Adams continued to seek a diplomatic solution. He sent three American envoys—John Marshall, Elbridge Gerry, and Charles Pinckney—to France in one last ditch effort to negotiate an end to the repeated provocations. They were supposed to meet with the foreign minister, Charles Maurice de Talleyrand-Périgord, but once in Paris, the American diplomats were virtually ignored. Finally, three French agents known secretly as X, Y, and Z, approached them and demanded a bribe as a precondition for an audience with Talleyrand. This diplomatic insult had the immediate effect of terminating all hopes for further negotiations. When news of the incident reached American shores, public opinion quickly became inflamed. The slogan, "Millions for defense but not one cent for tribute," rallied the populace against France and prompted President Adams to inform Congress, "I will never send another minister to France without assurances that he will be received, respected, and honored as the representative of a great, free, powerful, and independent nation."[39]

The pro-French Democratic-Republicans were dismayed by the sudden turn of events, but they remained deeply suspicious of Adams. Convinced that the incident had been inflated to provide an excuse to go to war, the party of Madison and Jefferson remained in vocal opposition to the administration. Adams continued to prepare the nation's defenses by creating a navy department and mobilizing a small provisional army as a precaution should the French make an aggressive move against Florida or Louisiana. Still, the president balked at asking Congress for an official declaration of war.[40]

Although the vast majority of Americans supported Adams and demanded retaliation to uphold the nation's honor, the partisan Democratic-Republican press viciously lampooned the president ("his Rotundancy"). The papers accused him unfairly of being a closet monarchist and Anglophile.[41] Compounding the domestic political situation was the fact that there were thousands French émigrés living in the United States who had fled the excesses of the revolution. They collectively joined with the Jeffersonians in trying to alter and influence American foreign policy in a way that would favor the French.

The masthead of *Porcupine's Gazette*. Published by William Cobbet under the pseudonym "Peter Porcupine," the pro-Federalist newspaper began printing on March 4, 1797, the day of John Adams's inauguration as the nation's second president. The porcupine symbolized the editor's sharp opinions and pointed comments.

The situation was precarious. The United States could ill afford to fight another war, especially against such a powerful enemy, but neither could the nation allow partisan passions to dictate foreign policy. Congress responded by passing the infamous Alien and Sedition Acts, which President Adams promptly signed. The laws gave the President extraordinary powers to expel dangerous foreigners and to arrest those who "utter[ed] or publish[ed] any false, scandalous, and malicious writing or writings against the government of the United States, or either house of the Congress of the United States, or the President of the United States."[42] The legislation clearly violated the principles articulated in the First Amendment and confirmed the worst fears of those who had anticipated such abuse from the federal government.

John Dawson, a Virginia member of the House wrote to James Madison on July 5, 1798, about the new legislation. "[The Sedition Act] exceeds any thing which has disgrac'd the present session, or the history of any country pretending to be free—what is to become of us I cannot tell, but think we are certainly ruind if the people do not come forward & exercise their rights."[43] Vice President Jefferson agreed that the crisis was grave and returned to Monticello in hopes that with "a little patience ... we shall see the reign of witches pass over, their spells dissolved, and the people recovering their true sight, restoring their government to its true principles."[44]

The Sedition Act, in particular, was seen by both Jefferson and Madison as a fundamental assault on the right of freedom of speech supposedly guaranteed in the First Amendment. The aim of the hated legislation seemed to be designed to curb legitimate political debate along with eliminating opposition to the Adams administration. The two Virginians began to collaborate on preparing an effective response to the new federal laws. To avoid the danger of their correspondance being intercepted and ultimately published by a pro-Federalist newspaper,

Madison and Jefferson decided to meet personally at Montpelier or Monticello to discuss their strategy.[45]

The state legislatures were the logical instruments by which to protest the constitutionality of the Alien and Sedition Acts. Jefferson agreed to write the resolution for the Kentucky legislature, while Madison would in turn draft Virginia's response. The authorship of both resolutions was a closely guarded secret to protect the writers from any possible retribution. Jefferson's draft of the Kentucky resolution was the more radical document. Although professing a devotion to the Constitution and to the union, Jefferson declared that the action by the Congress was unconstitutional, and he was the first to raise the specter of potential state nullification of federal law. The document said, in part, "that the several states who formed that instrument, being sovereign and independent, have the unquestionable right to judge of its infraction; and that nullification, by those sovereignties, of all unauthorized acts done under colour of that instrument, is the rightful remedy."[46] The idea that an individual state could unilaterally negate a federal law was alarming and, in effect, the opening of a Pandora's Box that would haunt the nation for generations, finally culminating on the battlefields of the American Civil War.

Madison agreed with Jefferson's overall assessment that the Alien and Sedition Acts were unconstitutional, but he balked at the idea of denying the supremacy of federal law, which was clearly established in the Constitution. Madison's Virginia Resolution was, as a result, the more thoughtful, moderate, and reasoned response to the political crisis. Passed by the General Assembly on December 21, 1798, the resolution clearly reaffirmed Virginia's commitment to the Constitution as well as its duty to oppose any unjust usurpation of power.

> *That this Assembly most solemnly declares a warm attachment to the Union of the States, to maintain which, it pledges all its powers; and that for this end, it is their duty, to watch over and oppose every infraction of those principles, which constitute the only basis of that union, because a faithful observance of them, can alone secure its existence, and the public happiness.[47]*

It went on to declare that Congress had by its "alarming infractions" and "exercises in like manner a power not delegated by the constitution" violated the founders' intent.[48]

The Virginia and Kentucky Resolutions were sent to the Congress in Philadelphia, and a few other states submitted their own petitions in opposition to the

Alien and Sedition Acts.[49] Still, the laws remained in effect, and some twenty-five individuals were arrested and prosecuted for their rabble-rousing, including Benjamin Franklin Bache, the publisher of the *Aurora*. This firebrand editor was charged with "libeling the President & the Executive Government, in a manner tending to excite sedition, and opposition to the laws, by sundry publications and republications"[50] in part, for calling President Adams "old, querulous, bald, blind, crippled, toothless."[51]

The political turmoil effectively terminated Madison's self-imposed retirement. He returned to the Virginia state legislature in 1799 and continued to organize the Democratic-Republican opposition with the intent of securing Jefferson's election to the presidency the following year. At the same time, key military setbacks for Napoleon benefited the United States, as the French government relented and agreed to receive newly appointed American ministers without restriction and in accordance with full diplomatic protocol.[52] The immediate foreign policy crisis had abated, and the threat of war was, for the moment, averted.

As the nation approached the dawning of a new century, its citizens paused to mourn the passing of General George Washington, who died at Mount Vernon on December 14, 1799. James Madison addressed the Richmond legislature on the occasion.

> *Death has robbed our country of its most distinguished ornament, and the world of one of its greatest benefactors. George Washington, the Hero of Liberty, the father of his Country, and the friend of man is no more. The General Assembly of his native state were ever the first to render him, living, the honors due to his virtues. They will not be the second, to pay to his memory the tribute of their tears.*[53]

The lull in the political bickering to honor the memory of the first president was unfortunately short-lived. The presidential election of 1800 was on the horizon, and it would become notable for its ferocity and bitterness. For the Democratic-Republicans, the election was seen as a referendum on the policies of John Adams and the Federalists, and Jefferson's narrow electoral win and subsequent election by the House of Representatives seemed to be a vindication of their position.

It was also the beginning of a new era in American history, symbolized by the fact that he became the first president to be inaugurated in the newly constructed federal capital, Washington, D.C. Extraordinary as well was that it was the first time in the nation's history that a president of an opposing party, despite fundamental political differences, freely handed over office in a peaceful transition of power. That this feat was accomplished freely and without violence was an extraordinary testament to the federal Constitution. As if by divine providence, the hated Sedition Act had expired the previous day removing one of the major sources of contention between the two political parties.

There was little pageantry associated with Thomas Jefferson's inauguration as the nation's third president. Republican principles emphasized simplicity and informality, so the president-elect walked from his boarding house to the Senate chamber.[54] There, newly appointed Supreme Court Chief Justice John Marshall administered the oath of office.[55]

Jefferson was not known for his public oratory and mumbled through his inaugural address. It was, nonetheless, a masterpiece of political logic and still is considered to be one of the most significant speeches in American history. Jefferson reaffirmed his commitment to the nation's republican principles and also attempted to heal the political rift that had developed over the previous decade. Jefferson proclaimed,

> But every difference of opinion is not a difference of principle. We have called by different names brethren of the same principle. We are all republicans, we are all federalists. If there be any among us who wish to dissolve this Union, or to change its republican form, let them stand undisturbed as monuments of the safety with which error of opinion may be tolerated, where reason is left free to combat it.[56]

He went on to emphasize that, in a republic, citizens should be free to pursue their own happiness with minimal interference from the government.

> Still one thing more, fellow citizens, a wise and frugal government, which shall restrain men from injuring one another, shall leave them otherwise free to regulate their own pursuits . . . and shall not take from the mouth of labor the bread it has earned. This is the sum of good government.[57]

The following day, Jefferson sent James Madison's appointment as secretary of state to the Senate for confirmation. He explained his reasons for the appointment in his official communiqué.

> Know Ye, That reposing especial trust and confidence in the patriotism, integrity and abilities of James Madison of Virginia, I have nominated, and, by and with the advice and consent of the Senate, do appoint him Secretary of State, and do authorize and empower him to execute and fulfill the duties of

that office according to law; and to have and to hold the said office with all
the powers, privileges and emoluments to the same of right appertaining unto
him the said James Madison during the pleasure of the President of the United
States for the time being.[58]

Madison, however, remained a Montpelier. His father had been in ill health and passed away on February 27, so James Jr. was preoccupied with settling the terms of the estate. It would be several weeks before he could leave for Washington to assume his official duties and he would not be sworn-in until May 2.[59]

For the first three weeks, James and Dolley lived at the Executive Mansion at the insistence of President Jefferson. Jefferson enjoyed the company and, as a widower, he soon came to depend upon Dolley to serve as the unofficial hostess for the government. Her charm, beauty, and decorum helped ameliorate some of the primitivism of the infant capital. As her biographer Catherine Allgor notes, it was Dolley Madison's "emphasis on civility, [that] she offered Americans an alternative to older, coercive models of governing ... [she] built coalitions and connections every week in her drawing room."[60]

As Jefferson's closest friend and most trusted adviser, Madison was indispensable as secretary of state as foreign intrigue and international diplomacy continued to command the president's attention. Jefferson's first term in office had been particularly successful, punctuated with the infant navy's military victories over the Barbary pirates, the doubling of the size of the United States by the Louisiana Purchase, and the substantial scientific accomplishments of Lewis and Clark's Corps of Discovery. But, by contrast, his second term was an unmitigated disaster, as the British and French continued to violate American shipping rights with impunity. Jefferson's insipid response was the self-imposition of the domestic embargo, the immediate impact of which was to send the American economy spiraling into a depression and to alienate the New England merchant class.

Jefferson gladly retired from the presidency in 1809 and returned home to Monticello in anticipation of a long retirement of solitude surrounded by his family and friends. He poignantly acknowledged, "Never did a prisoner, released from his chains, feel such relief as I shall in taking off the shackles of power."[61]

The secretary of state, James Madison, was the obvious political successor to Jefferson. He was elected to the presidency in 1808, solidly defeating the Federalist candidate, Charles Cotesworth Pinckney. Madison's triumph was clouded by the inheritance of a vast array of problems, most notably a complex foreign policy impasse with no obvious solution. As president, he hoped that, by continuing to pursue a policy of economic coercion, Britain and France would be compelled to accept America's legitimate neutrality rights and global mercantile interests.[62] This would avoid a costly and dangerous war, which, as Edward Coles acknowledged, would be essentially an irrational act and "[a] savage and brutal manner of settling disputes."[63]

Madison was fully aware that any onset of hostilities would pose a grave threat to the nation's republican form of government. "Of all the enemies to public liberty," Madison once wrote, "war is, perhaps, the most to be dreaded, because it comprises and develops the germ of every other. War is the parent of armies; from these proceed debts and taxes; and armies, and debts, and taxes are the known instruments for bringing the many under the domination of the few."[64] Furthermore, once public opinion was aroused against a perceived enemy, all reason and political restraint would be quickly abandoned and, moderation would be replaced by fanaticism and fury.

It was certainly debatable as to which nation, Britain or France, was the more culpable for the continuing foreign policy predicament. Thomas Jefferson astutely observed from his mountain sanctuary in Charlottesville, "Bonaparte hates our government because it is a living libel on his, [and] the English hate us because they think our prosperity filched from theirs."[65] Nathaniel Macon, a congressman from North Carolina, concurred with this sentiment claiming that "the Devil himself could not tell which government, England or France, is the most wicked."[66] Yet to fight both offending and powerful countries simultaneously was suicidal, and, Madison understood, "to go to war against both, presents a thousand difficulties."[67]

But as despicable as Napoleon was, there were few military options available to the United States. Over the years, the French had been virtually stripped of their North American colonies by treaty, revolution, and war and were now primarily a continental European power, albeit with a strong and aggressive navy. The British, though, were a more available, accessible, and immediate enemy. For thirty years, they had stubbornly refused to accept American independency and continually preyed upon the nation's merchant fleet. Moreover, the British navy had forcibly impressed an estimated 5,000 sailors during the period from 1807 through 1812, forcing American seamen into involuntary service.[68] At the same time, British military leaders in Canada were suspected of inciting Indian hostilities and encouraging "a warfare which is known to spare neither age nor sex and to be distinguished by features peculiarly shocking to humanity."[69] American settlers on the frontier lived in a constant state of fear and through their western congressmen were demanding that the federal government take substantive and affirmative action on their behalf.

By 1812 it was apparent that there would be no successful diplomatic solution to the ongoing difficulties. With Napoleon preoccupied by his eastward invasion of Russia, the British represented the preeminent threat to the United States. The Virginia House of Delegates formally concluded, "The period has now arrived when peace, as we now have it, is disgraceful, and war is honorable."[70]

Under Article I, Section 8 of the United States Constitution, the power to declare war was reserved to Congress.[71] Madison, in his war message to the federal legislature, acknowledged that it "is a solemn question, which

"The British and their worthy allies." The British and French both violated American neutrality rights during the Jefferson and Madison administrations. The British were seen as the more culpable of the two because of their continued impressment of American sailors and their alleged provocation of Indian hostilities on the frontier.

the Constitution wisely confides to the Legislative Department of the Government."[72] The president went on to provide Congress with a lengthy chronology of British provocations and an indictment of "the conduct of her Government [by] a series of acts hostile to the United States as an independent and neutral nation,"[73] continuing,

> *British cruisers have been in the continued practice of violating the American flag on the great high way of nations, and of seizing and carrying off persons sailing under it ... violating the rights and the peace of our Coasts. They hover over and harass our entering and departing Commerce.[74]*

Madison did not exonerate the French from culpability, but only Britain was accessible to American military forces because of their continued presence in Canada.

The vote for war was divided along political and sectional lines, but Madison's resolution for war successfully passed both houses of Congress. The majorities were slim, however, with a seventy-nine to forty-nine vote in favor in the House of Representatives and just a nineteen to thirteen approval in the Senate. For the second time in just three decades, the United States was at war with the world's most powerful empire.

In truth, the nation was ill prepared for such a conflict. Republican sensibilities had distained standing armies, so there was only a small professional force augmented by various state militias of questionable reliability. Furthermore, the small American navy, although skillfully commanded, was woefully outnumbered and outgunned by the British. To make matters even worse, the Federalists remained steadfast in their opposition to the war, and soon a pamphlet by John Lowell was published, which forever branded the conflict as Mr. Madison's War.[75] The greatest advantages that the United States enjoyed were its geographic isolation and Napoleon's continued troublemaking in Europe. The French emperor necessarily commanded the primary attention of British military resources.

There were many battles and skirmishes, with America's greatest successes coming on the Great Lakes. The war was in stalemate until 1814, when the British surprised American forces by launching a summer offensive against the capital

"The taking of the city of Washington in America." The War of 1812 was deemed by its opponents as "Mr. Madison's War." In 1814, the British routed American defensive forces and looted and burned the nation's capital. The war ended a few months later with the signing of the Treaty of Ghent and a defacto return to the *status quo antebellum.*

of Washington, D.C. Advancing by barrages up the Chesapeake Bay and Patux-
ent River, the British soldiers were met by an American force at Bladensburg.
President Madison rode out to the battlefield and watched in horror as the city's
defenders were completely routed. There was little to do but abandon the capital.

Dolley Madison remained at the Executive Mansion, anxiously awaiting news
from her husband. She could hear the cannon fire in the distance. In a letter
written to her sister, Dolley recounted the day's events.

> *Since sunrise I have been turning my spy glass in every direction and watch-*
> *ing with unwearied anxiety, hoping to discern the approach of my dear husband*
> *and his friends, but, alas, I can descry only groups of military wandering in all*
> *directions, as if there was a lack of arms, or of spirit to fight for their own fire-*
> *sides! ... Our kind friend, Mr. Carroll, has come to hasten my departure, and is*
> *in a very bad humor with me because I insist on waiting until the large picture*
> *of Gen. Washington is secured, and it requires to be unscrewed from the wall.*
> *This process was found too tedious for these perilous moments; I have ordered*
> *the frame to be broken, and the canvass taken out it is done, and the precious*
> *portrait placed in the hands of two gentlemen of New York, for safe keeping.*
> *And now, dear sister, I must leave this house, or the retreating army will make*
> *me a prisoner in it, by filling up the road I am directed to take. When I shall*
> *again write you, or where I shall be tomorrow, I cannot tell!![76]*

Paul Jennings, Madison's personal servant, remembered the events somewhat
differently in his 1865 memoir, although he by no means discounts Dolley Madison's heroism or direction to remove the famous Gilbert Stuart painting.

> *It has often been stated in print, that when Mrs. Madison escaped from the*
> *White House, she cut out from the frame the large portrait of "Washington*
> *(now in one of the parlors there), and carried it off. This is totally false. She*
> *had no time for doing it. It would have required a ladder to get it down. All*
> *she carried off was the silver in her reticule, as the British were thought to be*
> *but a few squares off, and were expected every moment. John Susé (a French-*
> *man, then door-keeper, and still living) and Magraw, the President's gardener,*
> *took it down and sent it off on a wagon, with some large silver urns and such*
> *other valuables as could be hastily got hold of. When the British did arrive, they*
> *ate up the very dinner, and drank the wines, &c., that I had prepared for the*
> *President's party.[77]*

The subsequent burning of the United States Capitol, the Executive Mansion, the Navy Yard, and other federal buildings was humiliating. Fortunately, the president and first lady, along with the members of the government, were able to escape, and the British were eventually turned back on September 14 at Fort McHenry in Baltimore.

The New England and Federalist opposition to Mr. Madison's War only increased with the military setbacks. In December 1814, delegates from five northern states met in Hartford, Connecticut, to discuss the progress of the war and the economic policies of both the Madison and Jefferson administrations. They proposed a series of Constitutional amendments designed to reduce the power of the southern states and to eliminate what they feared was becoming a Virginia presidential "dynasty."[78] The amendments included provisions for the abolishment of the Three-fifths Compromise, establishing a one-term limit for the president, requiring a two-thirds majority to declare war, and a mandate that a president's successor must come from a state different than his own.[79]

The Hartford Convention proved to be one of the most ill-timed meetings in American history. Although unknown to the delegates, the Treaty of Ghent ending

"The Hartford Convention or Leap No Leap." In December 1814, Federalist opponents of the War of 1812 met in Hartford to propose several substantive amendments to the Constitution. It proved to be one of the most ill-timed political gatherings in history and accelerated the eventual decline and extinction of the Federalist Party.

the War of 1812 had been signed on December 24, making the Hartford Convention irrelevant and giving it the appearance of being disloyal. The treaty defined no victor and was, in effect, a return to the *status quo antebellum*. The fighting ended shortly thereafter (although the Battle of New Orleans occurred after the Treaty had been signed and made Andrew Jackson a national hero). America had survived its second war with Great Britain and preserved its independence. The Federalist Party never recovered from the Hartford Convention and would be able to mount only one more campaign for president before disappearing forever.[80]

For Madison, the War of 1812 had been a triumph of his republican principles. It had preserved America's honor and reaffirmed the nation's independence, all without any suppression of liberty or individual rights. As Benjamin Lear noted, there had not been "one trial for treason, or even one prosecution for libel."[81] Madison was hailed for conducting the war "without the sacrifice of civil or political liberty ... without infringing a political, civil, or religious right."[82] In 1817, John Adams wrote to Thomas Jefferson that, "notwithstand[ing] a thousand faults and blunders, [James Madison's] Administration has acquired more glory, and established more Union, than all his three Predecessors, Washington, Adams and Jefferson, put together."[83]

ENDNOTES

Epigraph: J.P. Brissot de Warville quoted in Irving Brant, *James Madison, Father of the Constitution: 1787-1800* (Indianapolis: The Bobbs-Merrill Company Inc., 1950), 232-233.

[1] George Washington to James Madison, November 17, 1788, in W. W. Abbot, ed., *The Papers of George Washington: September 1788-March 1789*, Presidential Series (Charlottesville: University Press of Virginia, 1987), 115

[2] Edward Carrington to James Madison, November 9, 1788, in Robert A. Rutland, ed. *The Papers of James Madison: 7 March 1788 - 1 March 1789*. Charlottesville: University Press of Virginia, 1977, 336.

[3] Rutland, *7 March 1788 - 1 March 1789*, xvii-xviii.

[4] Richard Henry Lee quoted in Brant, *Father of the Constitution*, 237.

[5] Mayer, *Son of Thunder*, 448.

[6] James Madison to George Washington, December 2, 1788, quoted in Abbot, 146.

[7] The word "gerrymandering" did not come into use until 1812. It was named after James Madison's vice president, Elbridge Gerry, who manipulated congressional districts for political gain while governor of Massachusetts.

[8] The counties in Madison's district were Albemarle, Amherst, Culpeper, Fluvanna, Goochland, Louisa, Orange, and Spotsylvania. Virginia had ten congressional districts; the number was designated in Article I, Section 2 of the Constitution. After 1790, the apportionment of congressional seats would be determined by the decennial census.

[9] Richard Labunski, *James Madison and the Struggle for the Bill of Rights* (New York: Oxford University Press, 2006), 152.

[10] James Madison quoted in Labunski, 155.

[11] James Madison quoted in Mayer, 451.

[12] The final vote tabulation was Madison 1,308 and Monroe 972. See Stuart Leibiger, *Founding Friendship: George Washington, James Madison, and the Creation of the American Republic* (Charlottesville: University Press of Virginia, 1999), 100. Richard Labunki's book, *James Madison and the Struggle for the Bill of Rights*, is an excellent resource on the Madison/Monroe election.

[13] Labunski, 184.

[14] William Maclay quoted in Kenneth R. Bowling and Helen E. Veit, ed., *The Diary of William Maclay and Other Notes on Senate Debates: March 4, 1789-March 3, 1791* (Baltimore: Johns Hopkins University Press, 1988), 5.

[15] James Madison quoted in Robert Morton Smith, 591.

[16] Joseph J. Ellis, *His Excellency: George Washington* (New York: Vintage Books, 2004), 185.

[17] Abbot, 153.

[18] George Washington, First Inaugural Address, quoted in Abbot, 176.

[19] Brandt, *Father of the Constitution,* 164-265.

[20] James Madison quoted in Philip B. Kurland and Ralph Lerner, eds., *The Founder's Constitution* (Chicago: University of Chicago Press, 1987), 20.

[21] James Jackson quoted in Kurland, 21.

[22] James Madison quoted in Kurland, 24.

[23] The original first two amendments dealt with enumeration in the House and congressional pay raises. Neither passed the state legislatures, so the twelve amendments were reduced to ten, which became known as the Bill of Rights.

[24] Richard B. Bernstein and Jerome Agel, *Amending America: If We Love the Constitution So Much, Why Do We Keep Trying to Change It?* (New York: Time Books, 1993), 39.

[25] Roger Sherman quoted in Bernstein, 42.

[26] Bernstein, 44-45.

[27] James Madison quoted in Peterson, 192.

[28] Thomas Jefferson to William Short, January 3, 1793, available at http://www.loc.gov/exhibits/jefferson/190.html.

[29] John Adams quoted in Brandt, *Father of the Constitution,* 457.

[30] James Madison quoted in Peterson, 204.

[31] George Washington's Farewell Address is available at: http://avalon.law.yale.edu.

[32] The state legislatures still determine the process for selecting electors for president. According to Article II, "Each State shall appoint, in such Manner as the Legislature thereof may direct, a Number of Electors, equal to the whole Number of Senators and Representatives to which the State may be entitled in the Congress." Today all of the states allow the people to vote for electors, but there is no Constitutional guarantee for a popular vote for president.

[33] Vermont, Kentucky, and Tennessee had been admitted to the union by 1796.

[34] Thomas Jefferson quoted in Peterson, 210.

[35] Madison to James Madison Sr., March 12, 1787, quoted in J.C.A. Stagg, ed., *The Papers of James Madison: 27 April 1795-27 March 1797* (Charlottesville: University Press of Virginia, 1989), 500.

[36] John Adams to Abigail Adams, January 14, 1797, in David B. Mattern, et al, ed., *The Papers of James Madison: 31 March 1797-3 March 1801* (Charlottesville: University Press of Virginia, 1991), xix.

[37] Brian T. Neff, "Fracas in Congress: The Battle of Honor between Matthew Lyon and Roger Griswold" available at http://etext.virginia.edu/journals/EH/EH41/Neff41.html.

[38] Madison to Thomas Jefferson, February 18, 1798, in Mattern, *Papers of James Madison,* 82.

[39] John Adams quoted in David McCullough, *John Adams* (New York, Simon & Schuster, 2001) 503.

[40] McCullough, 499.

[41] The newspapers of the era were openly partisan. The Federalist editor of *Porcupine's Gazette* explained, "PROFESSIONS OF IMPARTIALITY I shall make none. They are always useless and are besides perfect nonsense … To profess impartiality here, would be as absurd as to profess it in a war between Virtue and Vice, Good and Evil, Happiness and Misery." Quoted in Hazel Dicken-Garcia, *Journalistic Standards and the Press's Role to 1850,* (Madison: University of Wisconsin Press, 1989), 99.

[42] The Alien and Sedition Acts and the Virginia and Kentucky Resolutions are available at http://avalon.law.yale.edu/subject_menus/alsedact.asp.

[43] John Dawson to James Madison, July 5, 1798, in Mattern, *Papers of James Madison,* 162.

[44] Thomas Jefferson quoted in Ketcham, *Madison: A Biography,* 394.

[45] Jefferson stopped at Montpelier on July 2 and 3, 1788, to speak with Madison. This was just a few days before the Sedition Act became law. Madison returned the visit by traveling to Monticello on October 15. Jefferson again visited Madison at his home on December 18 and March 7, 1799. See Mattern, *Papers of James Madison,* xxvii.

[46] Kentucky Resolution available at http://avalon.law.yale.edu/subject_menus/alsedact.asp.

[47] The Virginia Resolution quoted in Mattern, *Papers of James Madison,* 189.

[48] Ibid., 189.

[49] Smith, 1072.

[50] Jeffrey L. Pasley, *The Tyranny of Printers: Newspaper Politics in the Early American Republic* (Charlottesville: University Press of Virginia, 2001), 98.

[51] Benjamin Frankin Bache quoted in Ketcham, *Madison: A Biography*, 393.

[52] McCullough, 527.

[53] James Madison quoted in Mattern, *Papers of James Madison*, 295.

[54] Bernard A. Weisberger, *America Afire: Jefferson, Adams, and the Revolutionary Election of 1800* (New York: HarperCollins Publisher, 2000), 9.

[55] John Marshall was one of President Adams's famous "midnight appointments." The outgoing chief executive made several important judicial appointments prior to leaving office. This outraged the incoming administration and led to the important Supreme Court case, *Marbury v. Madison*, which defined the principle of judicial review. Marshall wrote the landmark opinion.

[56] Thomas Jefferson quoted in Weisberger, 281.

[57] Ibid., 283.

[58] Thomas Jefferson quoted in James Morton Smith, 1172-1173.

[59] Ketcham, *Madison: A Biography*, 389-390.

[60] Catherine Allgor, *A Perfect Union: Dolley Madison and the Creation of the American Nation* (New York: Henry Holt and Company, 2006), 9-10.

[61] Thomas Jefferson quoted in Ketcham, *Madison: A Biography*, 466.

[62] Americans found economics to be a powerful weapon during the colonial period. During the Stamp Act and subsequent political crises, associations, non-importation agreements, and boycotts proved effective in getting Britain to change its imperial policies. Such economic coercion remains a cornerstone of contemporary American foreign policy.

[63] Edward Coles quoted in Ketcham, *Madison: A Biography*, 530.

[64] James Madison quoted in David B. Mattern, ed., *James Madison's "Advice to My Country"* (Charlottesville, University Press of Virginia, 1997), 106.

[65] Thomas Jefferson quoted in Ketcham, *Madison: A Biography*, 504.

[66] Nathaniel Macon quoted in Ketcham, *Madison: A Biography*, 524.

[67] James Madison quoted in Ketcham, *Madison: A Biography*, 526.

[68] Borneman, 48.

[69] James Madison quoted in Stagg, 436.

[70] Borneman, 49.

[71] There have been five declared wars in American history—the War of 1812, the Mexican War, the Spanish-American War, World War I, and World War II. There was a unanimous consensus only for World War II (only Congresswoman Jeanette Rankin of Montana, a confirmed pacifist, voted against Franklin Roosevelt's request for a declaration of war). Since 1945, virtually all military involvements have been a product of executive policy, including the Korean, Vietnam, and Iraq conflicts.

[72] James Madison quoted in Stagg, 437.

[73] Ibid., 432.

[74] Ibid., 432-435.

[75] John Lowell's pamphlet, titled *Mr. Madison's War. A Dispassionate inquiry into the reasons alleged by Mr. Madison for declaring an offensive and ruinous war against Great-Britain. Together with some suggestions as to a peaceable and constitutional mode of averting that dreadful calamity. By a New-England farmer,* is available at http://www.archive.org/details/mrmadisonswar00lowe. The Library of Congress also maintains an extensive Web site with primary source materials on the War of 1812 at http://www.loc.gov/rr/program/bib/1812/.

[76] Dolley Madison to Lucy Payne Washington Todd, August 23, 1824, in Allgor, 193-194.

[77] Jennings, 12-13.

[78] The Three-fifths Compromise inflated Southern representation in the House of Representatives. The Federalists feared that Virginia would continue to dominate the presidency. Four of the first five presidents came from the commonwealth.

[79] Robert A. Rutland, ed., *James Madison and the American Nation: An Encyclopedia* (New York: Charles Scribner's Sons, 1994), 183-186.

[80] Rufus King was the last Federalist candidate for president. He lost to James Monroe by an electoral margin of 183 to 34.

[81] Benjamin Lear quoted in James Morton Smith, 1761.

[82] Ibid.

[83] John Adams quoted in James Morton Smith, 1761.

CHAPTER SIX

Gradualism, Compensation, and Colonization

Mr. Madison … was one of the best men that ever lived. I never saw him in a passion, and never knew him to strike a slave. — PAUL JENNINGS

The summer of 1783 was a difficult period for James Madison, despite good foreign and domestic news. The fighting in the Revolutionary War had virtually ceased after George Washington's impressive victory at Yorktown, and public sentiment was growing to demobilize American military forces. There was also promising news that a formal peace treaty with Great Britain recognizing American independence was imminent and that several of the states were already in the process of re-establishing commercial relations with England. It had been more than three years, though, since Madison had been home to Virginia and to his beloved Montpelier. During this period of self-imposed exile, he had been forced to endure many personal difficulties, including the inconvenience of living in Philadelphia with several of his fellow congressmen in a modest boardinghouse located on the corner of Fifth and Market Streets. Things got progressively worse for Madison when, in June, the entire congress was forced to evacuate the confederation capital to avoid the wrath of angry, inebriated American soldiers who were in mutiny over the failure of the government to pay them back wages for their military service. Congress meekly reconvened on June 26 in the nearby city of Princeton, New Jersey. The change of venue to the home of his alma mater held no nostalgia or joy for the thirty-two-year-old, who was once again in frail health. He found the new working conditions abominable and the accommodations primitive.[1] Madison somberly wrote, "In this village the public business ... [cannot] be conveniently done ... [We] were extremely put to it to get any quarters at all, and are at length put into one bed in a room not more than 10 feet square ... without a single accommodation for writing."[2]

On a more personal level, Madison was still trying to recover emotionally from the sudden and unexpected news that his fiancée, Kitty Floyd, had unilaterally ended their brief engagement. While on a trip to New York, she had whimsically fallen in love with another man, abruptly destroying all of Madison's hopes and dreams for returning to the Virginia piedmont with a new bride and a life of marital bliss. His friend, Thomas Jefferson, attempted to console Madison in a personal letter written from Monticello.

> *I sincerely lament the misadventure which has happened, from whatever cause it may have happened. Should it be final however, the world still presents the same & many other resources of happiness, and you possess many within yourself, firmness of mind & unintermitting occupations will not long leave you in pain, no event has been more contrary to my expectations, and these were founded on what I thought a good knowledge of the ground, but of all machines ours is the most complicated & inexplicable.*[3]

With his term in Congress set to expire in early November, a serious situation further complicated Madison's personal affairs. His personal slave, Billey, was refusing to return with him to Montpelier.[4]

By all accounts, Billey was a loyal and faithful servant who had accompanied Madison to Philadelphia in 1780. But once removed from the regionalism of Virginia's plantation society, he was able to experience firsthand the genuine fervor and patriot spirit that were sweeping the country. The newspapers and broadsides during the Revolution were filled with letters and editorials denouncing British tyranny and proclaiming the inalienable rights of man. Patriot leaders spoke openly of the dawning of a new epoch of liberty and freedom. Moreover, within Philadelphia, there was a pervasive anti-slavery sentiment among its citizens, and the city had become the center of a robust and energetic abolitionist movement. All of these factors undoubtedly had a profound impact upon Billey and increased his determination to live the remainder of his life as a free man.

Madison quickly realized that there was actually very little that he could do to compel Billey to go back with him to Virginia. Force was not an option, and his servant was so enamored and enthused with patriot sentiments that if he were to return, he would pose a serious threat to the outward tranquility of the Montpelier estate by exposing the other slaves to the ideals of the American Revolution. The results would certainly be disastrous and would make the other slaves aware of their own lamentable conditions.[5] This could only lead to anger, bitterness, widespread discontent and even the potential of open revolt. Madison acknowledged the situation in a somber letter to his father.

> *On a view of all circumstances I have judged it most prudent not to force Billey back to Va. Even if could be done; and have accordingly taken measures for his final separation from me. I am persuaded his mind is too thoroughly tainted to be a fit companion for fellow slaves in Virga. The laws here do not admit of his being sold for more than 7 years. I do not expect to get near the worth of him; but cannot think of punishing him by transportation merely for coveting that liberty for which we have paid the price of so much blood, and have proclaimed so often to be the right, & worthy the pursuit, of every human being.[6]*

An artist's rendition of the south yard at Montpelier. Slaves lived at various locations throughout the Montpelier plantation. Tobacco was the major source of wealth in Virginia, and most enslaved individuals were engaged in its cultivation and production. James Madison personally owned approximately one hundred slaves at any given time.

Madison, like most enlightened individuals of his era, was convinced that slavery was immoral and wrong. It was, in essence, America's original sin, and slavery would continue to taint the nation's history as long as it was allowed to exist. Likewise, the very presence of a large, enslaved population within the country exposed the Revolutionary Generation to charges of hypocrisy and tarnished their gleaming rhetoric and self-righteous pronouncements about natural rights and the evils of tyranny. Madison openly acknowledged that slavery was "an evil, moral, political, economic, and sad blot on our free country."[7]

It is thus shocking that Madison, a man who keenly understood the foibles of human nature and who had studied the intricacies of ancient and modern governments, could find no realistic solution for ending the institution of slavery during his lifetime. As historian Ralph Ketcham notes, Madison's "writings and speeches are laced with moral and political condemnations of the institution— it simply could not be reconciled with his earnest republican ideology. Yet he never acted effectively against slavery nor separated himself from the political system sustaining it."[8] There were, admittedly, no easy or obvious answers to the dilemma of slavery, and few Southern plantation owners were willing to risk their economic fortunes for a moral principle. As Early Lee Fox posits in *The American Colonization Society*, "Why did not the slaveholding States at this time abolish slavery? Because they did not know how; because the abolition of slavery was the greatest problem the South had ever been called on to face; because no man had suggested a plan that seemed capable of execution."[9]

In many ways, as long as his father lived, the younger Madison was insulated from the day-to-day realities of being a southern plantation owner. The Montpelier estate was a massive agricultural and industrial operation. It consisted of thousands of acres of tobacco and wheat fields and had more than thirty separate buildings, including a blacksmith shop and a distillery operation. All of it was owned and operated by James Madison Sr.[10]

The elder Madison managed the plantation's sizeable slave population, roughly one hundred fifty people at its peak. He directed their labor, but overseers usually supervised their daily work, thus avoiding much direct contact with the plantation's many fieldhands. Still, in Douglas Chambers' words, "James Madison Sr. was someone who demanded respect"[11] and, of course, obedience from his workers. There were some occasions when he was forced to intervene directly with major problems, such as when a disgruntled runaway would flee the estate. In one such instance, Madison took out an advertisement in a Richmond newspaper.

Run away … a Mulatto Slave, named Anthony, about 17 years old, low, but well made, had very light hair and grey eyes;…he has been used to house business, and as a waiting servant. Ten Dollars Reward will be given, if he be secured so that I get him again … It is probable he has secured a pass, or a Certificate of his Freedom; and has changed his name and clothes. James Madison [Sr.].[12]

The entire Madison family's wealth and social privilege was directly dependent upon its enslaved population. A youthful James Madison's fanciful wish "to depend as little as possible on the labor of slaves"[13] was little more than hyperbole. It was slavery that freed James Madison to pursue his academic studies; it was slavery that allowed him the time for public service; and it was slavery that sustained him in his comfortable lifestyle. In a remarkably candid letter written by his wife, Dolley, in 1818, she admitted as much.

"Sukey has made so many depredations on every thing, in every part of the house that, I sent her to black Meadow last week but find it terribly inconvenient to do without her, & suppose I shall take her again, as I feel too old to undertake to bring up another—so I must even let her steal from me, to keep from labour myself."[14]

Because of his many elective offices and his desire for public service, Madison was repeatedly absent from his Montpelier home for extended periods of time. From 1776 until his retirement from the presidency, the longest time that he was in continual residence at Montpelier was the period from 1797 through 1801. This was the interregnum when John Adams and the Federalist Party were in the ascendancy and controlled the federal government. But even during this blissful time of semi-retirement, Madison remained interested, active, and involved in politics. He continued to write and was carefully orchestrating a plan to help Thomas Jefferson win the presidency in the next election. During this brief period of domesticity, Madison used the opportunity to renovate the estate's manor house, expanding and transforming it into a duplex, thereby strategically separating his parents from his own household while residing in the same building. Virtually all of the manual labor was done by slaves.

In February 1801, Thomas Jefferson's election to the presidency was finally secured after a bitter and intense political campaign and an equally contentious electoral controversy played out in the House of Representatives.[15] With the inauguration rapidly approaching, James Madison became the logical choice for the new administration's secretary of state. On February 27, however, Madison's father

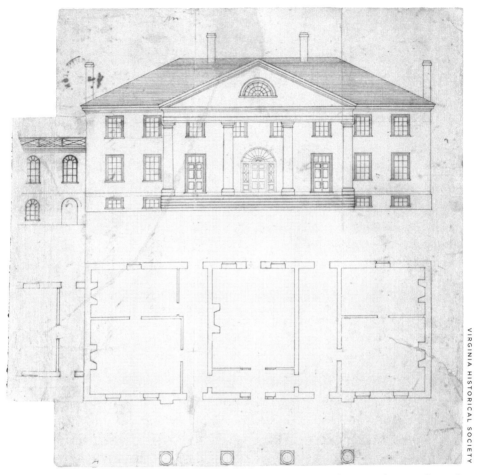

Joiner James Dinsmore's architectural drawing of Montpelier. Madison enlarged and modernized the Montpelier manor house on several occasions. In the 1790s, he converted the structure temporarily into a duplex with separate facilities and private living accommodations for his parents. Madison's father died in 1801, while his mother, Eleanor "Nelly" Conway Madison, lived until 1829.

died at Montpelier, necessitating that he delay his journey to the new capital of Washington, D.C. As the eldest son, Madison was the obvious choice to inherit the main Montpelier estate, but the rest of his father's will proved outdated and complicated, with numerous handwritten amendments. These contributed to the confusion and uncertainty over the senior Madison's final testament. As the chief executor of the will, James was responsible for working out its details, including the painful process of dividing up the plantation's slaves among the family members.[16] On March 7, he wrote an apologetic letter to President Jefferson.

Since my last which went by the mail in course, the papers of my deceased father have been opened. His will was made thirteen years ago, since which two of my brothers have died, one of them leaving a large number of children mostly minors, and both of them intestate. The will itself, besides the lapsed legacies, does not cover all the property held at the time; & valuable parcels of property were acquired subsequent to the will. The will is also ambiguous in some important points, and will raise a variety of questions for legal opinions if not controversies.[17]

Madison was at last able to leave Montpelier for Washington on April 27, and he was sworn in as the nation's fifth secretary of state five days later. He was destined to remain in public office over the ensuing sixteen years and would thus once again be primarily an absentee landowner. Montpelier's daily plantation operations and the fate of its slaves were to be, once again, left in the hands of overseers.

During his tenure as both secretary of state and president, Madison would make brief periodic visits to his home, particularly during the brutally hot summer months when Washington, D.C., was transformed into a malarial swamp. During these visits, he was able to directly review the state of affairs on his plantation. Even then, government business had to remain his top priority. In 1817, Madison retired from more than thirty years of almost continuous public service, comfortable in the knowledge that the immediate fate of the republic was finally secure. He now was able to focus his attentions more clearly upon the damaging implications of slavery on the nation's character acknowledging that "the magnitude of this evil among us is so deeply felt and so universally acknowledged; that no merit could be great than that of devising a satisfactory remedy for it."[18]

The United States was rapidly changing during the early nineteenth century. The spirit of the Enlightenment, which had had such a profound influence upon Madison, was quickly fading as America's Revolutionary Generation gradually died out. Both would soon be consigned to the annals of history, only to be replaced by a new breed of American politicians. These young, brash, and impatient men had no direct memory of the hardships and struggles for independence, nor of the difficulties inherent in the establishment of a new republican form of government. Instead, they were proud nationalists, eager for power, who openly courted the public's favor. They also demanded westward expansion to the Pacific in fulfillment of America's "manifest destiny." In so doing, they were unknowingly the primary force responsible for bringing slavery to the forefront of the national political debate, as each territory's application for admission to the union renewed the contentious argument over whether it should be free or slave.

James Madison watched all of these developments from his Montpelier retreat with dismay. He was certain that there was no immediate or obvious solution for the deeply entrenched system of slavery. Existing for almost two hundred years in North America by James Madison's time, slavery continued to grow and expand with the passage of time. There could be no realistic end to the pernicious institution, Madison believed, unless the following conditions occurred—no matter how implausible or unlikely. "A general emancipation of slaves ought to be," Madison maintained, "1. Gradual. 2. Equitable & satisfactory to the individuals immediately concerned. 3. Consistent with the existing & durable prejudices of the nation."[19] To Madison, an immediate abolition of slavery simply was not plausible. As historian Virginia Moore notes, Madison "did not believe that emancipation, under present conditions, would benefit black people much, if at all; freed slaves were at too great a disadvantage in a white man's society."[20]

Madison thought that any voluntary process of emancipation in the United States would take several generations to complete, in part because he felt that it was only equitable and fair that slaveholders be financially compensated for the loss of their "property." He recognized that this would be an enormously expensive proposition for the infant republic, but insisted that such an effort be undertaken at the sole expense of the national government. In a letter written in 1819, Madison explained, "If slavery as a national evil is to be abolished, and it be just that it be done at the national expence, the amount of the expence is not a paramount consideration."[21]

The economic strain caused by a future emancipation could be ameliorated somewhat through the sale of vast tracts of the nation's western lands.[22] Madison carefully calculated that with approximately one and a half million slaves then living within the United States, at a cost of an average four hundred dollars per slave, it would take a sum of about six million dollars to financially compensate their owners. Madison figured hypothetically: "This will require 200 mils, of Acres at 3 dollrs. Per Acre; or 300 mils, at 2 dollrs. Per Acre a quantity which tho' great in itself, is perhaps not a third part of the disposable territory belonging to the U.S. And to what object so good so great & so glorious, could that peculiar fund of wealth be appropriated."[23]

But even the emancipation of slaves and the corresponding compensation of their owners was still not enough for Madison. He advocated a simultaneous program of colonization, a systematic and organized process to relocate newly freed slaves somewhere else. This was predicated upon his belief that racial animosity had become so deeply ingrained in the country's culture that it precluded the races from living peacefully together.[24] Madison wrote that such a relocation program was necessary "to be consistent with existing and probably unalterable prejudices in the U.S." He continued, "The freed blacks ought to be permanently removed beyond the region occupied by or allotted to a white population."[25] Ironically, it was here on this most critical of issues where Madison's legendary intellectual genius failed him. It instead reduced him to a parochial man of his time and location, unable or unwilling to grasp the incredible moral and ethical implications of such a brutally inhumane policy.

Madison was a determined and lifelong supporter of colonization; he remained oblivious to the many facts and numerous statistics that exposed its folly. At the very end of his presidency, he became one of the founding members of the American Colonization Society. It was established in December 1816, originally as the American Society for Colonizing the Free People of Color of the United States, and its membership was impressive. Included among its supporters were some of the nation's most notable luminaries—Daniel Webster, James Monroe, Henry Clay, Francis Scott Key, John Marshall, Bushrod Washington, William Crawford.[26] The society's avowed purpose was to establish a new colony in western Africa, specifically in Liberia, as a suitable place to relocate former slaves after emancipation. The society would have the additional benefit of serving as a convenient political forum for both northerners and southerners, who could meet regularly to discuss the issue of slavery dispassionately. Together, it was hoped, these wise men would be able to help develop a national remedy for it. There would be no effort to consign blame for the existence of slavery; the society's members gladly accepted the fact that the system had been inherited from their forefathers, thereby exonerating the current generation. In 1829, Union College President Eliphalet Nott explained their sentiments.

> *Our Brethren of the South have the sympathies, the same moral sentiments, the same love of liberty as ourselves. By them, as by us, slavery is felt to be an evil, a hindrance to our prosperity, and a blot upon our character. But it was in being when they were born and has been forced upon them by a previous generation.*[27]

Daniel Dana of New Hampshire went further: "The guilt is strictly national … National, then, let the expiation be."[28]

Despite their early optimism, the society was predestined to become an abysmal failure. Its membership failed to grasp the harsh demographic realities of the nation. With the Constitutionally mandated abolition of the international slave trade in 1808, the vast majority of the nation's huge slave population was domestically born, and most slaves were able to claim an American lineage that stretched back for generations. They had no direct knowledge of their earlier African heritage and shared American characteristics and customs, including language.

Further adding to the society's difficulties was the fact that its colony, Liberia, was a wholly artificial place, created out of convenience and imagination rather than upon any logic or cultural history. Virtually none of the emancipated slaves scheduled for deportation from the United States had any ancestral roots or connections to the region. There were no efforts to take into consideration linguistic or cultural origins, and, as a result, few slaves had any desire to resettle in a distant foreign land. The famed English writer, Harriet Martineau, who visited Madison at Montpelier during her grand tour of the United States, recounted that, in her conversations with the former president, he openly acknowledged this fact. She wrote of "their horror of going to Liberia, a horror which [Madison] admitted to be prevalent among the blacks, and which appears to me decisive as to the unnaturalness of the scheme."[29]

Still, Madison effusively praised the efforts and goals of the American Colonization Society. For some unexplained reason, he considered its efforts to be the only viable alternative for ending slavery within the United States, as he said in a 1819 letter.

> *The experiment under this view of it, merits encouragement from all who regard slavery as an evil, who wish to see it diminished and abolished by peaceable & just means; and who have themselves no better mode to propose. Those who have most doubted the success of the experiment must at least have wished to find themselves in an error.*[30]

The ordinary domestic growth among America's enslaved population further doomed any international colonization effort. Extant documents and records from the society showed that from 1825 through 1836, only thirty-three hundred freed slaves were relocated to Liberia. During roughly the same period, the official U.S. census recorded that the country's slave population had increased by more than five hundred thousand people.[31] These statistics and figures were readily available at the time, especially to a scholar of Madison's stature. Yet the stark and undeniable numbers had surprisingly little effect upon his thinking, Harriett Martineau recalled.

> *With regard to slavery he owned himself almost to be in despair. He had been quite so till the institution of the Colonization Society. How such a mind as his could derive any alleviation to its anxiety from that source is surprising.*

I think it must have been from his overflowing faith; for the facts were before him that in eighteen years the Colonization Society had removed only between two and three thousand persons, while the annual increase of the slave popula-tion in the United States was upward of sixty thousand.[32]

In 1833, in one of the final political acts of his life, Madison agreed to serve as the American Colonization Society's president, despite the fact that he was eighty-two years old, in declining health, and a virtual invalid. He was, though, in sound mind when he wrote from Montpelier that it was his "earnest prayer, that every success may reward the labors of an Institution … so noble in its object of removing a great evil from its own country."[33] When Madison died just three years later, despite his obvious financial difficulties, he still left the substantial sum of two thousand dol-lars to the society in his will. It amounted to a final act of utter futility.[34]

The inefficiency of the slave labor system had plagued and frustrated Madison throughout his entire lifetime. He knew full well that an enslaved labor force was intrinsically less efficient than one that employed free wage earners. Slaves had no desire or incentive to be productive, since additional work resulted in few tangible benefits for themselves or for their families. A slave's life was already hard enough, consisting of an endless repetition of planting, weeding, and harvesting, with the years defined only by the perpetual cycle of the seasons. It was only natural that the slave community would constantly subvert the system by feigning illness, breaking farm equipment, petty theft, and other subterfuge. Paul Jennings recounted Madi-son's reaction to such acts of defiance, writing, "Whenever any slaves were reported to him as stealing or 'cutting up' badly, he would send for them and admonish them privately, and never mortify them by doing it before others."[35] Auguste Levas-seur confirmed this in 1824 when he accompanied Lafayette to Montpelier.

I will not enter into particulars concerning the management of Mr. Madison's plantation: it is exactly what might be expected from a man distinguished by good taste and love of method, but unable to employ other labourers than slaves; who, whatever may be their gratitude for the good treatment of their master, must always prefer their own present ease to the increase of his wealth.[36]

The profitability of slaveholding was further called into question by the need to support a large labor force regardless of their capacity to work. Southern planta-tion owners were responsible for feeding, clothing, and housing all of their slaves, regardless of their age or condition. It was an incredibly expensive proposition and one that Madison acknowledged was slowly and steadily bankrupting him. The

1830 U.S. Census revealed that, although Madison owned 106 slaves, thirty-six percent of them were under the age of ten and thus unable to do any substantive work. Another nine were over the age of fifty-five; two were blind. In reality, Madison's most productive slaves constituted less than half of Montpelier's enslaved population, hardly a prescription for prosperity.[37] Harriet Martineau recorded that Madison "found, by the last returns from his estates, that one-third of his own slaves were under five years of age. He had parted with some of his best land to feed the increasing numbers, and had yet been obliged to sell a dozen of his slaves the preceding week."[38] Madison even would acknowledge the stark reality that a typical ten-acre farm in Pennsylvania was more productive than his own two thousand-acre estate. Regardless of these indisputable facts and fiscal realities, however, the slave system was destined to remain unchallenged and unchanged at Montpelier.[39]

The moral contradictions of slavery were also apparent to Madison; perhaps no more so than by the fact that his wife, Dolley, who had been raised a Quaker, was somehow able to make the transition from the religion's strong, anti-slavery position to that of being a mistress of an active slave plantation. In 1783, Dolley's father, in a conspicuous and courageous act of faith and conscience, freed all of his slaves and relocated his entire family from Hanover County, Virginia, to live in the free city of Philadelphia.[40] Just a few years later, after Dolley married the Episcopalian Madison, she was expelled from her Quaker church, and she adopted not only her husband's faith, but became a slaveholder as well. Dolley Madison "had become," according to historian David Mattern, "the wife of a slave-owning

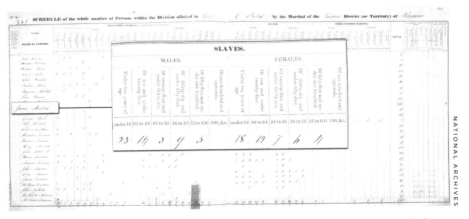

The 1830 Census. The federal census recorded that James Madison owned 106 slaves, forty-one of whom (or thirty-six percent) were under the age of ten. The system was inefficient, and Madison was convinced that it was slowly bankrupting him.

Virginia planter, moving from the provincial world of observant Quakers to the cosmopolitan world of politics, affluence, and gaiety."[41] Apparently Dolley shared few of her parents' qualms of conscience over the institution of slavery. As historian Rosemarie Zagarri notes, "Despite her Quaker origins, Dolley never once expressed a moral objection to slavery. Her approach to buying and selling slaves seems matter-of-fact, simply a matter of economic necessity."[42] James Madison would later confide to Harriet Martineau in 1835, that Southern women

> *cannot trust their slaves in the smallest particulars, and have to superintend the execution of all their own orders; and they know that their estates are surrounded by vicious free blacks, who induce thievery among the negroes, and keep the minds of the owners in a state of perpetual suspicion, fear, and anger.*[43]

The moral depravity of slavery and its corrupt practices would forever trouble Madison, although not enough to end the practice at Montpelier. The system, by its very nature, demanded that young slave girls remain continually pregnant since every birth of every child would ostensibly increase a plantation owner's wealth. Madison was disgusted by this practice and all of its implications, Martineau recounted. "With regard to slavery [Madison] owned himself almost to be in despair ... acknowledging, without limitation or hesitation, all the evils with which it has ever been charged ... every slave girl being expected to be a mother by the time she is fifteen."[44] Even more troublesome to Madison was the reality that many white plantation owners freely took sexual liberties with their female slaves, thereby exerting their ultimate power over them as well as populating the commonwealth with thousands of mixed-race, fatherless children. Even James Madison's closest friend, Thomas Jefferson, was accused of having fathered several children by his slave mistress, Sally Hemings.

Madison would never publicly or privately comment on the numerous allegations and rumors about Jefferson's behavior. Jefferson's political allies and even his later biographers were eager to dismiss the widely circulating charges as the spurious accusations of his political opponents. One of the purveyors of such questionable fare was James Callendar, a disgruntled and notorious alcoholic, who seemed to fit nicely into this stereotype. Still, his contentions made their way into the Virginia newspapers.

> *It is well known that the man, whom it delighteth the people to honor, keeps, and for many years past has kept, as his concubine, one of his own*

slaves. Her name is SALLY. The name of her eldest son is TOM. His features are said to bear a striking although sable resemblance to those of the president himself. The boy is ten or twelve years of age. His mother went to France in the same vessel with Mr. Jefferson and his two daughters. The delicacy of this arrangement must strike every person of common sensibilities. What a sublime pattern for an American ambassador to place before the eyes of two young ladies! By this wench Sally, our president has had several children ... the AFRICAN VENUS is said to officiate, as housekeeper at Monticello.[45]

Jefferson's extended family, who was living with him at Monticello during his retirement years, was complicit in the general denial of such gossip. Jefferson's grandson, Jeff Randolph, did admit, though, that there were slaves at Monticello who bore a startling resemblance to the plantation's patriarch, as historian Alan Pell Crawford writes in *Twilight at Monticello.*

At least one of these house slaves looked so much like Jefferson himself, Jeff Randolph told the biographer Henry S. Randall, that 'at some distance in the dusk the slave, dressed in the same way, might have been mistaken for Mr. Jefferson.' On one occasion, Jeff said, a dinner guest 'looked so startled as he raised his eyes from [Jefferson] to the servant behind him, that his discovery of the resemblance was ... perfectly obvious to all.' Only Jefferson himself 'never betrayed the least consciousness of the resemblance,' Jeff Randolph said.[46]

Adding to the complexity of this historical riddle was the fact that one of Sally's sons, Madison, officially claimed Jefferson's paternity in the 1870 national census. The census taker recorded, "This man is the son of Thomas Jefferson."[47] Hemings further alleged in the *Pike County Republican* that he had been named at birth for James Madison at the insistence of Dolley during one of the couple's many visits to Monticello.

As to myself, I was named Madison by the wife of James Madison, who was afterwards President of the United States. Mrs. Madison happened to be at Monticello at the time of my birth, and begged the privilege of naming me, promising my mother a fine present for the honor. She consented, and Mrs. Madison dubbed me by the name I now acknowledge, but like many promises of white folks to the slaves she never gave my mother anything. I was born at my father's seat of Monticello, in Albemarle County, Va., near Charlottesville, on the 18th day of January, 1805.[48]

Although the passage of time has made it impossible to fully document and authenticate Madison Hemings' statement, there is some circumstantial evidence to provide credence to his claim. James and Dolley Madison were, in fact, at Monticello from September 9 through 16, 1804, during the time of Sally's pregnancy.[49] Moreover, Madison Hemings was undoubtedly personally convinced that his story, which had been conveyed to him through a strong African-American oral tradition, was true. He even went so far as to name his only son after James Madison. Even more significant are the results of scientific DNA testing conducted in 1998 on both the Jefferson and Hemings descendants. These indicate with a high probability that Thomas Jefferson fathered most of Sally's children, including Madison.[50]

There are, though, others who have significant doubts about Dolley Madison's alleged role in this historical conundrum. The leading historians and scholars at the Thomas Jefferson Memorial Foundation believe that Sally probably chose the name for her child independently but they acknowledge that there is "no way to document why or under what circumstances she made that decision."[51] Leni Sorenson further points out the strong emotional connection to the story that exists within the Hemings family. "Because 'a promised gift that is never fulfilled' is a common theme in many African American family

A page from Thomas Jefferson's farm book indicating the "Roll of Negroes 1810." Jefferson's wife had died in 1781, after which he was alleged to have taken a slave as a mistress and fathered several mixed-race children, including Madison Hemings. Born in 1805, Madison Hemings declared that he was indeed Jefferson's son and that he was named for James Madison by Dolley Madison.

oral histories," she explains, "it is clear that whites not living up to responsibilities continued to carry a psychological weight."[52]

Whatever hopes James Madison may have had that a common, national consensus for the peaceful ending of slavery would eventually take place forever evaporated in 1831. On New Year's Day, William Lloyd Garrison published the first issue of his abolitionist newspaper, the *Liberator*. The paper would be relentless and uncompromising in its condemnation of slavery and of all of its practitioners.

> *I will be harsh as truth, and uncompromising as justice. On this subject, I do not wish to think, or speak, or write, with moderation. No! No! Tell a man whose house is on fire to give a moderate alarm; tell him to moderately rescue his wife from the hands of the ravisher; tell the mother to gradually extricate her babe from the fire into which it has fallen;—but urge me not to use moderation in a cause like the present. I am in earnest—I will not equivocate—I will not excuse—I will not retreat a single inch—AND I WILL BE HEARD.*[53]

In an instant, Garrison's inflammatory rhetoric polarized emotions throughout the country, branding slavery as a clear moral evil. The South quickly mobilized to mount its own defensive position, developing an equally passionate oratory devoted to rationalizing and justifying the region's so-called "peculiar institution." Plantation owners and planters felt betrayed by the North, and matters became progressively worse just a few months later, when a charismatic slave named Nat Turner led a group of slaves on a bloody rampage through Southampton, Virginia. His renegade band indiscriminately slaughtered sixty-one men, women, and children on eleven different farms. The slave rebellion was widely reported throughout the nation and reinforced plantation owners' fears of a potential uprising among their own slaves. It was altogether more alarming because these horrors were perpetrated in a locale where the slaves lived in close proximity to their owners (rather than on large plantations). They knew one another, and the enslaved population was generally assumed to be passive and loyal. The seeming randomness and viciousness of the murders was terrifying to whites, especially in districts where the slaves outnumbered their white owners (this was true in Madison's home county of Orange).[54] The "bloody butchery," as the *Richmond Compiler* reported, was widespread. "[The rebellious slaves] were mounted to the number of 40 or 50; and with knives and axes—knocking on the head, or cutting the throats of their victims ... Not a white person escaped, at all of the houses they visited, except *two*!"

The events in southern Virginia sparked a contentious debate within the state legislature, many arguing for the swift removal of all freed blacks from the state.[55] For James Madison, though, Nat Turner's rebellion confirmed his belief that colonization was necessary. In 1833, Madison received two predictable pro-slavery pamphlets from Professor Thomas Dew of the College of William and Mary. These popular leaflets evidenced the rapidly growing shift in Southern attitudes toward justifying slavery as a positive good. Madison politely responded to Dew, first apologizing for "the feebleness incident to my great age," but then clearly expressed his disagreements for the sentiments conveyed in the literature.

> In the views of the subject taken in the pamphlet, I have found much valuable and interesting information, with ample proof of the numerous obstacles to a removal of slavery from our country, and everything that could be offered of its continuance ... but I am obliged to say, that in not a few of the data from which you reason, and in the conclusion to which you are led, I cannot concur.[56]

Madison then elaborated on the conditions necessary for the deportment of slaves and reiterated the desirability of Africa as the primary site for such relocations.

When Madison died in 1836, the sectional divisions between North and South had widened into an ever-increasing chasm. There would be no peaceful end to

LIBRARY OF CONGRESS

The "Horrid Massacre" Broadside. In 1831, a charismatic Nat Turner led an unsuccessful slave rebellion in southern Virginia, killing some 61 people. The incident terrified Southerners and, coupled with a more activist abolitionist movement, accelerated an increase in sectional divisions.

slavery in the United States. The American Colonization Society, a product of human conceit and foolishness, slipped, forgotten and unmourned, into bankruptcy and ruin.[57]

For James Madison's slaves, though, their peril was more imminent. The death of an owner meant that his slaves were listed among his many assets and could be sold to alleviate any accumulated debt. Historian Douglas Chambers, in *Murder at Montpelier*, recounts the slaves' reaction to Madison's death and burial.

> ... *when the casket was lowered in to the yawning grave, and the minister intoned the final line, 'dust to dust,' as [James] Barbour remembered. 'the hundred slaves gave vent to their lamentations in one violent burst that rent the air.' Though Barbour and the other whites may have attributed this outburst of grief to the loss of 'a kind and indulgent master,' the slaves may also have been grieving their own impending ruin. Within a decade, the African American community at Montpelier would be broken up, and by 1850 most of the slaves were dispersed ... the death of President Madison marked the beginning of the old community's ruination.[58]*

The slave community's fears were justified. Dolley Madison was soon forced to deal with a dire financial situation, which was exacerbated by her son's fondness for alcohol and ever-mounting gambling debts. Edward Coles recounted that slave traders descended like vultures upon Montpelier.

> *Reports had gotten abroad that she (Mrs. Madison) wished to sell many of them (her slaves) & every day or two (while I was at her house in Aug.) a Negro trader would make his appearance, & was permitted to examine the Negroes. It was like the hawk among the pigeons. The poor creatures wd run to the house & protest agt being sold, & say their old master had said in his Will that they were not to be sold but with their consent. She sold while I was with her a woman & 2 children to her Nephew Ambrose Madison who lives near her. The woman protested agt. being sold & the more so as her Husband was not sold with her. Mr Madison's course has been most unfortunate for his memory, & for the peace & happiness of his Widow, as it respects his Slaves; & can only be accounted for by a change of his intention towards them in the last year or 2 of his life. He had sold three farms, & refusing to part with one of his slaves, brought them all to the Montpellier farm, where they had been for many years too numerous for the cultivation of his land, & were literally exhausting that & impoverishing him-*

self. Whilst he often dwelt on this state of things, he would as uniformly declare his determination not to sell them; & had often intimated his intention, long before he avowed his determination to me, to emancipate them. About 2 years ago he wrote me an explanatory letter about his having finally brought himself to sell 16 to a kinsman, with their own consent. He has now died without having freed one—no not even Paul—& has left so many more than can be judiciously employed on his estate that his poor Widow is compelled, it is said, to sell many of them. Thus he has imposed on his Widow a most painful task, one which he ought to have performed himself.[59]

Ultimately, destitute and in financial ruin, Dolley was forced to sell everything, including the Montpelier slaves.

Slavery was Madison's greatest personal and political failure. He had no realistic solution for a system that he fully acknowledged corrupted the nation's founding principles. It would ultimately lead the United States into a brutal civil war and the slaughter of more than six hundred thousand citizens and to a lingering legacy of injustice and mistrust.

When Madison's servant, Billey, refused to return to Montpelier in 1783, it was no mere act of defiance—it was, in essence, his own declaration of independence—a clear indictment of slavery. Billey assumed the name William Gardner and became a successful merchant, living as a free man in Philadelphia.[60] In 1795, he was lost at sea while on a voyage to New Orleans. Madison wrote a remarkably detached letter to his father asking him to inform Billey's enslaved parents of his death.

You may let Old Anthony & Betty know that their son Billey is no more. He went on a voyage to N. Orleans, where being sick as were most of the crew, & very weak under the operation of a dose of physic, he tumbled in a fainty fit overboard & never rose.[61]

Old Anthony and Betty were destined to die as slaves and were buried at Montpelier having never tasted the freedom that had so captured their son's imagination.

Today the many visitors to Madison's home find the grounds well manicured and serene. His restored mansion dominates the beautiful landscape, and its interiors glisten from fresh plaster and paint. The horse tracks located on the grounds are in perpetual use with jockeys exercising well pampered thoroughbreds. Located in a small grove of trees just a short way from the archaeological foundations of the original Mount Pleasant homestead are two modest historical markers that indicate the presence of a graveyard. There are no headstones or

LINDA BOUDREAUX MONTGOMERY

An artist's rendition of a slave funeral at Montpelier. The slave cemetery today is only modestly commemorated with two historical markers. The individual graves remain unmarked and unidentified.

monuments to mark the individual burials, however, just slight indentions in the earth or an occasional strategically placed rock. These are the graves of many of James Madison's slaves. They remain nameless in death and virtually anonymous to history. Yet it was their collective toil and labor that freed James Madison and his contemporaries to contemplate the great political issues of the era. With their lives they helped create the new American Republic.

ENDNOTES

Epigraph: Paul Jennings, *A Colored Man's Reminiscences of James Madison* (Brooklyn: George C. Beale, 1865), 15. The full quotation reads: "Mr. Madison, I think, was one of the best men that ever lived. I never saw him in a passion, and never knew him to strike a slave, although he had over one hundred; neither would he allow an overseer to do it. Whenever any slaves were reported to him as stealing or "cutting up" badly, he would send for them and admonish them privately, and never mortify them by doing it before others. They generally served him very faithfully."

[1] Hutchinson, *The Papers of James Madison: 3 May 1783-10 February 1784*, xxxvii. Between June 30 and November 2, Madison attended fewer than half of the sessions of the Confederation Congress.

[2] Madison quoted in Ketcham, *Madison: A Biography,* 142.

[3] Thomas Jefferson to James Madison, August 31, 1783, in Hutchinson, *Papers of James Madison,* 298.

[4] Chambers, *Murder at Montpelier,* 131. Chambers includes an excellent census of the Madison slaves. In Appendix C, he identifies Billey's parents as Old Anthony and Betty and notes that, after manumission, Billey married Henrietta, who worked for Thomas Jefferson, 211-212.

[5] Theodore M. Whitfield, *Slavery Agitation in Virginia: 1829-1832* (New York: Negro Universities Press, 1930), 10-11.

[6] Madison to James Madison Sr., September 8, 1783, in Hutchinson, *Papers of James Madison,* 304.

[7] Madison quoted in *Letters and Other Writings,* cited by Daniel Horton, senior essay: *Admiring Failures: An Examination of James Madison's Attitudes Towards Slavery and His Attempts to Eliminate It,* (Harrisonburg: James Madison University, 2008).

[8] Ralph Ketchum, ed., *Selected Writings of James Madison,* The American Heritage Series (Indianapolis: Hackett Publishing Company Inc., 2006), xxviii.

[9] Early Lee Fox, The *American Colonization Society 1817-1840,* (Baltimore: The Johns Hopkins Press, 1919), 15.

[10] Chambers, 129-130.

[11] Ibid., 125.

[12] Runaway Slave ad, Ketcham, 374-375.

[13] Madison to Edmund Randolph, July 26, 1785, in Rutland, *Papers of James Madison: 10 March 1784-28 March 1786,* 327-328.

[14] Dolley Madison to Anna Cutts, July 23, 1818, in David B. Mattern and Holly C. Shulman, eds., *Selected Letters of Dolley Payne Madison* (Charlottesville: University of Virginia Press, 2003), 231.

[15] Due to a structural quirk in the Electoral College system, Thomas Jefferson and Aaron Burr received the same number of votes. The election was thrown into the House of Representatives, where it took 36 ballots before Jefferson was finally selected as president on February 17, 1801.

[16] Chambers, 134.

[17] Robert J. Brugger, ed., *The Papers of James Madison: 4 March-31 July 1801,* Secretary of State Series (Charlottesville: University of Virginia Press, 1986), 6.

[18] Madison to Francis Wright, September 1, 1825, in Mattern, *Advice to My Country,* 99.

[19] Madison to Robert Evans, June 15, 1819, in Peterson, *Biography in His Own Words,* 371.

[20] Virginia Moore, *The Madisons: A Biography* (New York: McGraw-Hill Book Company, 1979), 88.

[21] James Madison to Robert Evans, June 15, 1819, in Peterson, 373.

[22] Moore, 475.

[23] Madison to Robert Evans, in Peterson, 372.

[24] Allan Yarema, *The American Colonization Society: An Avenue to Freedom* (Lanham: University Press of America, 2006), 17.

[25] Madison to Robert Evans, in Peterson, 372.

[26] Yarema, vii, and Fox, 9.

[27] Eliphalet Nott quoted in Fox, 16.

[28] Daniel Dana quoted in Fox, 13.

[29] Harriet Martineau, *Retrospect of Western Travel,* (Armonk: M.E. Sharpe, 2000), 76.

[30] Madison to Robert Evans, in Peterson, 372.

[31] The 1820 census placed the U.S. slave population at 1,538,022. Ten years later, it had increased to 2,009,043.

[32] Martineau quoted in Peterson, 377.

[33] Madison quoted in P. J. Staudenraus, *The African Colonization Movement: 1860-1865* (New York: Octagon Books, 1980), 183.

[34] Yarema, 25.

[35] Jennings, 15.

[36] Auguste Levasseur quotations, *Slavery at Montpelier,* National Park Service, available at http://www.nps.gov/nr//twhp/wwwlps/lessons/46montpelier/46facts2.htm.

[37] Find the 1830 Census at the National Archives and Records Administration. Madison's entry appears on p. 321 of the census devoted to Virginia and to Orange County.

[38] Ibid., 377.

[39] Moore, 475.

[40] Mattern, 12. Additionally, in a 31 August 1834 to Margaret Bayard Smith, Dolley Madison recounts, "My family are all Virginians except myself, who was born in N. Carolina whilst my Parents were there on a

visit of one year, to an Uncle. Their families on both sides, were among the most respectable and they, becoming members of the society of friends soon after their Marriage manumitted their Slaves, and left this state for that of Pennsylvania, bearing with them their children to be educated in their religion—I believe my age at that time was 11." Dolley Payne Todd Madison to Margaret Bayard Smith, 31 August 1834, in Holly Shulman, ed., *The Dolley Madison Digital* Edition (Charlottesville: University of Virginia Press, Rotunda, 2004), http://rotunda.upress.virginia.edu/dmde/DPM0796 (accessed 2008-09-05).

[41] Ibid., 17.

[42] Rosemarie Zagarri, review of *The Selected Letters of Dolley Payne Madison,* by Holly C. Shulman, ed., *Journal of the Early Republic 24,* no. 1 (Spring 2004): 136-138.

[43] Martineau, 76.

[44] Martineau quoted in Peterson, 377.

[45] James Callendar in the *Recorder* quoted in Michael Durey, *"With the Hammer of Truth": James Thomson Callender and America's Early National Heroes,* (Charlottesville: University of Virginia Press, 1990), 158.

[46] Crawford, *Twilight at Monticello,* 139.

[47] 1870 Census, NARA, Roll M593-1263, page 699.

[48] Madison Hemings quoted in *Pike County Republican* 1873: http://www.pbs.org/wgbh/pages/frontline/shows/jefferson/cron/1873march.html.

[49] M. Hackett, ed., *Papers of James Madison: 1 September 1804-31 January 1805,* Secretary of State Series (Charlottesville: University of Virginia Press, 2007), xxxix. A timeline of Madison's life during this period is available here.

[50] The Thomas Jefferson Foundation maintains an extensive website devoted to the Jefferson-Hemings controversy. The entire DNA report is available at http://www.monticello.org/plantation/hemingscontro/hemingsresource.html. It concludes, in part: "The DNA study, combined with multiple strands of currently available documentary and statistical evidence, indicates a high probability that Thomas Jefferson fathered Eston Hemings, and that he most likely was the father of all six of Sally Hemings's children appearing in Jefferson's records. Those children are Harriet, who died in infancy; Beverly; an unnamed daughter, who died in infancy; Harriet; Madison; and Eston."

[51] Leni A. Sorensen, "Madison Hemings Naming." E-mail to Philip Bigler. March 5, 2008. Sorenson continues, "However, because 'a promised gift that is never fulfilled' is a common theme in many African American family oral histories it is clear that whites not living up to responsibilities continued to carry a psychological weight."

[52] Ibid. One year later, Jefferson's daughter gave birth to James Madison Randolph, the first child ever born at the Executive Mansion in Washington. The personal circumstances of Madison's two namesakes were remarkably different—one born a slave and the other into a life of privilege and advantage.

[53] William Lloyd Garrison quoted in Marc M. Arkin, "The Federalist Trope: Power and Passion in Abolitionist Rhetoric," *The Journal of American History* 88, no. 1 (2001): 75.

[54] Kenneth S. Greenberg, ed., *The Confessions of Nat Turner and Related Documents* (The Bedford Series in History and Culture. Boston: Bedford Books of St. Martin's Press, 1996), 3-6. Nat Turner was not captured for several weeks, but once arrested, tried, and convicted, he was executed. His body was skinned and his skull was put on display until it mysteriously disappeared. The population of Orange County in 1830 comprised 6,456 whites and 7,983 slaves. Statistics are available at http://fisher.libvirginia.edu/collections/stats/histcensus.

[55] J. Cromwell, "The Aftermath of Nat Turner's Insurrection," *The Journal of Negro History* 5, no. 2 (1920): 223.

[56] James Madison to Thomas Dew February 23, 1833, quoted in Gaillard Hunt, ed., *The Writings of James Madison, comprising his Public Papers and his Private Correspondence, including his numerous letters and documents now for the first time printed* (New York: G. P. Putnam's Sons, 1900), 319.

[57] Staudenraus, 224-225.

[58] Chambers, 128-129.

[59] Edward Coles to Sarah (Sally) Coles Stevenson, November 12, 1836, in Shulman, *Dolley Madison Digital Edition.* http://rotunda.upress.virginia.edu/dmde/DPM2827 (accessed 2008-09-08).

[60] Ketcham, 374.

[61] Madison to James Madison Sr., December 1795, in J.C.A. Stagg, ed., *The Papers of James Madison: 27 April 1795-March 1797,* (Charlottesville: University of Virginia Press, 1989), 174.

CHAPTER SEVEN

Liberty, Learning, and Legacy

His name will descend to posterity with that of our illustrious Washington. One achieved independence, and the other sustained it.—What proud and happy feelings will he carry with him to that retirement to which he will also carry the acclamations and the prayers of a grateful nation. — TOAST GIVEN BY BENJAMIN LEAR TO JAMES MADISON ON JULY 4, 1816

In 1829, Andrew Jackson was inaugurated as the seventh president of the United States. He was hailed by many Americans as the champion of the common man, the first chief executive popularly elected by the people, who were increasingly being entrusted by their state legislatures to vote for the slates of presidential electors.[1] Jackson had already earned a well-justified reputation as a man with keen leadership skills, but he also possessed a tempestuous temper and the uncanny ability to hold a grudge. For James Madison, now living in quiet retirement at Montpelier, Jackson's election to the highest office in the land signified the end of an entire era in American history. The Enlightenment that had so dominated American political thought and ideology throughout the eighteenth century and that had shaped the thinking of such men as Madison and Jefferson was clearly over; it had been replaced by a growing sense of egalitarianism, democracy, sectionalism, and incivility. No longer would the nation expect to be routinely governed by a wise, natural aristocracy of dispassionate patriots who placed the public good above their own personal popularity and nobly sacrifice their own self-interest for the nation's well-being. Instead, individuals like Andrew Jackson—aggressive, uncompromising, and certain in their own infallibility— would personify the antebellum period in the United States.

Throughout the entire country, this new breed of populist politician was coming to power at both the state and national levels. For these individuals, the American Revolution was not a memory, but rather a distant event in history, something to read about, study, even admire. Few Americans truly comprehended the danger in undertaking the revolution or appreciated the miracle that was the American republic. As James Madison well knew, success had not been pre-ordained or inevitable. An elderly John Adams acknowledged the marvel in an 1818 letter. "The complete accomplishment of [the American Revolution], in so short a time and by such simple means, was perhaps a singular example in the history of mankind. Thirteen clocks were made to strike together—a perfection of mechanism, which no artist had ever before effected."[2] The Revolutionary

PHILIP BIGLER

The ruins of Menokin, the ancestral home of Francis Lightfoot Lee. Madison spent his later years presiding as the last of the great founding generation as both the Enlightenment and the tobacco plantation era that had shaped him slipped away. All around him, America was rapidly changing. The nation was turning more democratic and populist, as personified by the election of Andrew Jackson to the presidency.

and Federalist periods had been, in fact, chaotic and confused, and those who survived them readily acknowledged their peril and uncertainty. Thomas Jefferson had noted without hyperbole in the Declaration of Independence that the founders were prepared to risk their lives, fortunes, and sacred honor to ensure freedom and liberty for future generations. They had done so in the face of considerable danger.

By the advent of the Jackson administration, the country's rapidly growing population was moving relentlessly westward in fulfillment of America's "manifest destiny." James Madison had been withdrawn from public life for more than a decade, although he still diligently read newspapers and pamphlets to follow the course of national events. He carefully monitored the nation's growing sectionalism and the divisions caused by the ever-present specter of chattel slavery.

By 1831, Madison was the sole survivor of America's remarkable founding generation—Jefferson was gone, Monroe was dying, and Washington, Adams, Hamilton and Henry were all in their graves. Somewhat sadly, Madison reflected, "Having outlived so many of my contemporaries, I ought not to forget that I may be thought to have outlived myself."[3] On March 16, Madison celebrated his eightieth birthday at Montpelier. Always frail and sickly, his health was rapidly deteriorating, amplified by painful rheumatism that was crippling his small frame. As Madison confided in a letter to Nicholas Trist, "I have been confined to my bed many days by a bilious attack. The fever is now leaving me but in a very enfeebled state, and without any abatement of my Rheumatism; which, besides its general effect on my health, still cripples me in my limbs, and especially in my hands and fingers."[4]

Before long, Madison's entire physical world was reduced to a small room, which was located immediately adjacent to his mansion's formal dining room. From the confines of his chair, though, he could still interact with the many guests to the estate and continue to enjoy robust conversations and even an occasional ribald joke or two. All who encountered Madison during this last period of infirmity remarked that although his body was failing, his intellect remained sharp and lucid undiminished by the ravages of time and age. Harriet Martineau described her 1834 meeting with the ailing Madison.

> *He had, the preceding season, suffered so severely from rheumatism, that, during this winter, he confined himself to one room, rising after breakfast, before nine o'clock, and sitting in his easy-chair till ten at night ... He com-*

plained of one ear being deaf, and that his sight, which had never been perfect, prevented his reading much, so that his studies 'lay in a nutshell;' but he could hear Mrs. Madison read, and I did not perceive that he lost any part of the conversation. He was in his chair, with a pillow behind him, when I first saw him; his little person wrapped in a black silk gown; a warm gray and white cap upon his head, which his lady took care should always sit becomingly; and gray worsted gloves, his hands having been rheumatic. His voice was clear and strong, and his manner of speaking particularly lively, often playful ... His relish for conversation could not have been keener.[5]

Madison became increasingly dependent upon the custodial care of his devoted and loving wife, Dolley. She described rarely leaving his side during this critical time, dutifully attending to his many needs. "I am occupied as usual with my husband and household—Mr. Madison being in the same feeble health and confinement."[6] In another letter, she wrote of her attention to his frail condition.

...my dear Husband has been in very bad health—and is still confined to the house with feebleness—resulting from a painful and diffusive Rheumatism—I have never left him half an hour, for the last two years—so deep is the interest, & sympathy, I feel for him! I look forward, however, with hope, to the genial season so near—for his restoration.[7]

Her hopes that Madison would eventually recover his health proved unrealistic. Now with his eyesight failing, Madison depended upon Dolley to read to him, and she continued to transcribe her husband's voluminous notes, which he had meticulously preserved from the Constitutional Convention. This editing was now of utmost priority since the publication of these valuable historical records upon Madison's death were expected to provide an ongoing source of income for his widow.

On June 28, 1836, the inevitable came, as James Madison, fourth president of the United States and Father of the United States Constitution, died quietly in his room at Montpelier. Paul Jennings, Madison's personal slave, was present and later recounted the final moments of Madison's mortal life.

I was always with Mr. Madison till he died, and shaved him every other day for sixteen years. For six months before his death, he was unable to walk, and spent most of his time reclined on a couch; but his mind was bright, and with his numerous visitors he talked with as much animation and strength of voice

as I ever heard him in his best days. I was present when he died. That morn-
ing Sukey brought him his breakfast, as usual. He could not swallow. His niece,
Mrs. Willis, said, 'What is the matter, Uncle James?' 'Nothing more than a
change of mind, my dear.' His head instantly dropped, and he ceased breathing
as quietly as the snuff of a candle goes out. He was about eighty-four years old,
and was followed to the grave by an immense procession of white and colored
people. The pall-bearers were Governor Barbour, Philip P. Barbour, Charles P.
Howard, and Reuben Conway; the two last were neighboring farmers.[8]

As was customary of the times, the funeral took place the following day. It was conducted in accordance with traditional Anglican rites. One of Madison's neighbors, Philip Barbour, recounted that during one point in the service, the gathered plantation slaves "gave vent to their lamentations in one violent burst that rent the air."[9] For all southern slaves, the death of an owner was a trau-matic event because it would have a direct impact on their fate. The unyielding and unknown terms of a master's last will and testament dictated the dispersal of his human property as well as his estate. Historian Douglas Chambers poi-gnantly notes, "Though Barbour and the other whites may have attributed this outburst of grief to the loss of 'a kind and indulgent master,' the slaves may also have been grieving their own impending ruin. Within a decade, the African-American community at Montpelier would be broken up, and, by 1850, most of the slaves would be dispersed."[10]

For the next two decades, James Madison's grave in the remote family cem-etery on the Montpelier grounds would remain unmarked while his alcoholic and inept stepson, Payne Todd, persisted in squandering the family's wealth and fortune. Todd callously ignored the societal need to erect a fitting monu-ment to the Father of the Constitution. Madison's extensive writings, however, the political philosophy they expressed, and his enduring faith in the Constitu-tion had already enshrined Madison in the pantheon of the early republic. Even more important than his place in American history, however, is James Madi-son's continuing relevance as the nation faces the challenges and ambiguities of the 21st century.

Knowledge will forever govern ignorance: And a people who
mean to be their own Governors, must arm themselves with the
power which Knowledge gives.

Throughout his life, Madison was widely recognized as the nation's preeminent political scholar. He reveled in books and exalted in the realm of ideas, believing in the necessity of developing informed opinions solidly grounded upon historical truth rather than rooted in whim, fantasy, or prejudice. His formal education, beginning with his study at Donald Robertson's school, was rigorous and demanding. He read serious and substantive books and carefully studied history in order to apply the valuable lessons of the past to the problems of contemporary society. As a student at the College of New Jersey (Princeton), Madison developed his lasting belief in the need for freedom of religion. This was, in essence, a commitment to the fundamental right to think for oneself, free from governmental interference, societal coercion, or public obstruction. In his words, "Opinions are not the objects of legislation,"[11] and true education was the noble quest for universal truth.

Confederate dead at Antietam. Despite Madison's final wish that "the Union of the States be cherished and perpetuated," sectional differences, slavery, and state's rights led to the American Civil War. Ironically, the bloodiest day in American history, the battle of Antietam, occurred on September 17, 1862, the seventy-fifth anniversary of the signing of the Constitution. The Union victory saved the Constitution, which, along with the Declaration of Independence and the Bill of Rights, remains a fundamental part of the American creed.

When Madison was preparing for the Constitutional Convention, he read voraciously, carefully studying, assessing, and analyzing the successes and failures of previous confederacies and other forms of government. It was his meticulous research, thoughtful analysis, and scholarly approach that led him to formulate the critical ideas that would shape the ensuing debate in Philadelphia. But, remarkably, Madison was never so entrenched in his beliefs that he could not be persuaded to compromise or even change his mind when confronted by superior evidence or argument. Although he initially opposed the inclusion of a Bill of Rights on the reasonable grounds that the Constitution's carefully enumerated and limited powers would prevent the federal government's intrusion into personal liberties, he eventually conceded the need for such amendments in order to pacify the opposition and to relieve public anxiety. Moreover, Madison then personally championed the cause of the Bill of Rights and skillfully crafted a series of appropriate amendments that would forever ensure the Constitution's integrity, while providing the desired overt guarantees of liberty. At the same time, Madison and the other delegates to the Constitutional Convention scrupulously evaded a troublesome debate over the morality of slavery, in effect passing the problem on to future generations. As Joseph Ellis writes in his outstanding book, *Founding Brothers*, "The distinguishing feature of the document when it came to slavery was its evasiveness. It was neither a 'contract with abolition' nor a 'covenant with death,' but rather a prudent exercise in ambiguity."[12] It would take the deaths of more than 600,000 Americans in the Civil War to finally end the iniquitous institution.

For James Madison and the founding generation, a well-educated, virtuous citizenry was essential for the preservation of liberty. "It is universally admitted that a well instructed people alone, can be permanently a free people,"[13] he explained. To help ensure this, during his first term as president, Madison proposed the creation of a national university to advance learning. In a speech to Congress in 1810 he argued that "a seminary of Learning ... would be universal in its beneficial effects. By enlightening the opinions, by expanding the patriotism; and by assimilating the principles ... sources of jealousy and prejudice would be diminished, the features of national character would be multiplied."[14] But the impending war with Britain prevented a national American university from ever becoming a reality. Madison, however, was undeterred and devoted much of his retirement in partnership with Thomas Jefferson to creating the University of Virginia. As he wrote in 1826, the university marked a fulfillment of his expressed faith in the importance of learning. "The best service that can be rendered to a Country, next to that of giving it liberty, is in diffusing the mental improvement equally essential to the preservation, and the enjoyment of the blessing."[15]

*The aim of every political constitution is, or ought to be, first,
to obtain for rulers men who possess most wisdom to discern, and most
virtue to pursue the common good of the society.*

The founders saw the American Revolution as a seminal event in human history—a triumph over arbitrary government, tyranny, and oppression. To them, the revolution was not an isolated, solitary event within the British Empire, but rather would serve as a powerful example to the rest of the world. Thomas Paine first expressed these sentiments in his pamphlet, *Common Sense*. "The cause of America is," he wrote, "in a great measure, the cause of all mankind."[16] Still, the American military victory at Yorktown in 1781 would be only the first step in the ultimate cause of liberty. It would take another sixteen years before the Constitutional Convention codified a new, republican form of government that would eventually provide the nation with stability and political viability.

The United States Constitution was, in fact, the product of the collective wisdom of the fifty-five delegates who attended the Philadelphia convention. Although James Madison would rightfully be conferred with the epithet of Father of the Constitution, he openly admitted that the government was not "the off-spring of a single brain. It ought to be regarded as the work of many heads and many hands."[17] This document, preserved in the National Archives, has remained the fundamental framework of the American government for more than two centuries, while its philosophy has informed and withstood wars, economic depression, political dissent, and domestic turmoil. There have been few structural changes to the government, a testament to the judgment and intelligence of its creators.[18]

Madison, unlike the more idealistic Thomas Jefferson, took a realistic and pragmatic view of human nature. He was not deceived by fanciful visions of an agrarian utopia and keenly understood man's predilection toward power and its enormous capacity for misuse. The federal system that Madison devised skillfully divided powers among the individual states as well as the three branches of the national government. An intricate system of checks and balances was intended to leave nothing to chance, for, as Madison observed, "All power in human hands is liable to be abused."[19] Abigail Adams was in concurrence with this somber assessment of human nature and wrote to her husband, John, "I am more and more convinced that man is a dangerous creature, and that power whether vested in many or few is ever grasping."[20]

The American government, despite common public misperception, was never intended to be a democracy. Madison realized that societal majorities could easily be as tyrannical as the most authoritarian and ruthless despot. Under the original provisions of the Constitution, only the House of Representatives was democratically elected by the people. The Senate was designed to serve the interest of the individual states, while the President was the sole figure to be selected by a national vote of the Electoral College.[21] This had the positive effect of insulating the government from the potential capriciousness of popular pressure.

Serious political disagreements were inevitable, but the founders were careful to distinguish between legitimate political discourse and personal attack. Although the debates were often fierce, substantive, and even ideological, there was a general acknowledgement that the opposition was well intentioned (with a few notable exceptions).[22] Madison and Monroe, while running against each other for Congress, campaigned together and maintained their personal friendship despite their considerable political disagreements. Even Madison's nemesis, Patrick Henry, was finally appeased with the adoption of the Bill of Rights. He wrote "that I will be sparing of Complaints against the Government, & find Fault as little as my fixed Habits of thinking will permit."[23] For James Madison, reasoned and civil debate along with mutual respect and compromise were essential to the overall health of the republic and were essential for promoting good government.

Where are his monuments? Where is his currency? Scholars generally like him, and today generally they like him more than Jefferson. Yet academic publications and scholarly conferences do not directly affect the public mind ... While Jefferson gives us license to determine what we want to be, Madison—more than any other member of the founding generation—made us what we are.

By 1836, the United States was politically polarized over the issue of slavery. Northern abolitionists were growing in strength and numbers, while their rhetoric was becoming increasingly strident. Southerners were defensive and angry, while any hopes for a realistic resolution to the nation's sectional differences were slowly abandoned. Madison was dismayed by this growing rift, and in 1834 he wrote what would be, in many ways, his final words of advice for the nation. Intended to be published only after his death, Madison's testament was

to be read as an honest and forthright statement, free from all political consid-
erations and influence.

> *"As this advice, if it ever see the light will not do it till I am no more it may
> be considered as issuing from the tomb, where truth alone can be respected, and
> the happiness of man alone consulted. It will be entitled therefore to whatever
> weight can be derived from good intentions, and from the experience of one who
> has served his country in various stations through a period of forty years, who
> espoused in his youth and adhered through his life to the cause of its liberty, and
> who has borne a part in most of the great transactions which will constitute
> epochs of its destiny."[24]*

Despite the ugly specter of sectionalism and slavery, Madison retained his sense
of optimism and fidelity to the United States Constitution.

> *The advice nearest to my heart and deepest in my convictions is that the
> Union of the States be cherished and perpetuated. Let the open enemy to it be
> regarded as a Pandora with her box opened; and the disguised one, as the Ser-
> pent creeping with his deadly wiles into Paradise.[25]*

The Constitution and the union would survive despite enormous obstacles and
even the American Civil War. But it remains incumbent upon each new generation to renew its commitment to the nation's founding principles and to James
Madison's enduring legacy.

In 1787, when Benjamin Franklin was leaving the final session of the Constitutional Convention, a citizen asked him what type of government America was
to have. He replied, "A Republic, if you can keep it."[26] That challenge remains
relevant to America's complex, technological society today. For the republic to be
preserved, the nation needs a well-informed, educated, and involved citizenry, as
well as an understanding of the principles of the Constitution and an apprecia-
tion of the essential James Madison.

ENDNOTES

Epigraph 1: Benjamin Lear quoted in Irving Brant, *The Fourth President: A Life of James Madison* (Connecticut: Easton Press, 1970), 407.
Epigraph 2: Madison to William Barry, August 4, 1822, in Mattern, 58.
Epigraph 3: Madison in Mattern, *Advice to My Country*, 62.
Epigraph 4: Robert M. S. McDonald, "The Madison Legacy: A Jeffersonian Perspective," *James Madison
and the Future of Limited Government.* J. Samples (Washington, D.C.: Cato Institute, 2002), 68.
[1] During the early nineteenth century, more and more states were allowing a popular vote for electors.

The first election in which it was a factor was the controversial election of 1824, which was ultimately decided by the House of Representatives. In the 1828 contest, Andrew Jackson received fifty-six percent of the popular vote and defeated his opponent, the incumbent president, John Quincy Adams by a 178-to-83 majority in the Electoral College. Presidential elections in the United States today are still determined by the electoral vote, with most states awarding their entire allotment of votes on a winner-takes-all basis. We have, in effect, fifty state elections (plus the District of Columbia, due to Amendment XXIII) for president. The national vote totals are irrelevant, although few contemporary Americans fully understand the constitutionally mandated process.

[2] John Adams to H. Niles, February 13, 1818, available at http://www.cooperativeindividualism.org/adams_john_american_revolution.html. (accessed 2009-01-05).

[3] Madison to Jared Spares, June 1, 1831, in Rakove, *Writings*, 858.

[4] Madison to Nicholas P. Trist, May, 1832, in Rakove, 859.

[5] Martineau, 74-75.

[6] Dolley Payne Todd Madison to Dolley Payne Madison Cutts, December 2, 1834, in Shulman, available at http://rotunda.upress.virginia.edu/dmde/DPM0783 (accessed 2008-12-08).

[7] Dolley Payne Todd Madison to Mary Elizabeth Payne Jackson Allen, February 25, 1834, in Shulman, available at http://rotunda.upress.virginia.edu/dmde/DPM0789 (accessed 2008-12-08).

[8] Jennings, 18-19.

[9] Ketchum, *James Madison: A Biography*, 670.

[10] Chambers, 129.

[11] Madison quoted in Mattern, *Advice to My Country*, 95.

[12] Joseph Ellis, *Founding Brothers: The Revolutionary Generation* (New York: Alfred A. Knopf, 2001), 93.

[13] Ibid., 40.

[14] Ibid.

[15] Madison to Littleton Dennis Teackle, March 29, 1826, in Mattern, 42.

[16] Thomas Paine, *Common Sense,* available at: http://earlyamerica.com/earlyamerica/milestones/commonsense/text.html.

[17] Madison to William Cogswell, March 10, 1834, in Mattern, 29..

[18] The Constitution has been amended only twenty-seven times. Eleven of the amendments (the Bill of Rights and Amendment XXVII) were written by James Madison.

[19] Madison to Thomas Ritchie, December 18, 1825, in Mattern, 80.

[20] Abigail Adams quoted in David McCullough, *John Adams,* (New York: Simon & Schuster, 2001), 101.

[21] Senators were chosen by the state legislature until the ratification of Amendment XVII in 1913. This progressive amendment granted the people the right to vote for their senators.

[22] The most notable exception to this was the duel between Alexander Hamilton and then-Vice President, Aaron Burr. Likewise, the brawl on the floor of the House between Roger Griswold and Matthew Lyon was a rare breech of personal decorum.

[23] Patrick Henry quoted in Mayer, 462.

[24] James Madison quoted in Rakove, *James Madison: Writings*, 866.

[25] Ibid.

[26] This story is credited to James McHenry, one of Maryland's delegates to the convention.

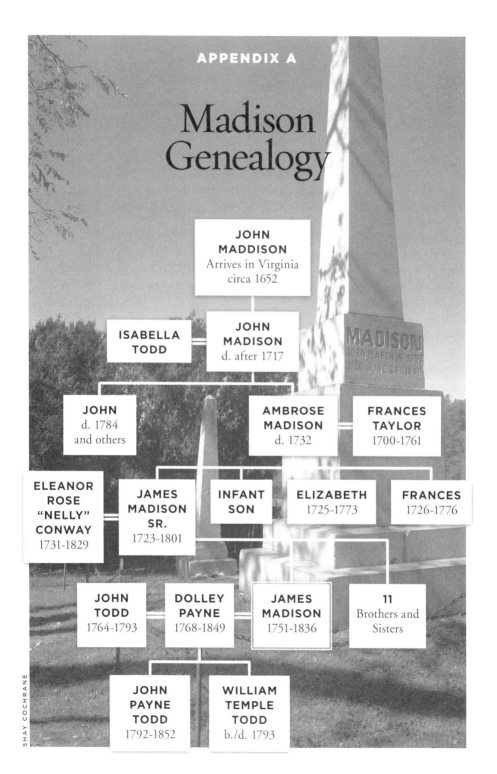

APPENDIX A

Madison Genealogy

JOHN MADDISON
Arrives in Virginia
circa 1652

ISABELLA TODD

JOHN MADISON
d. after 1717

JOHN
d. 1784
and others

AMBROSE MADISON
d. 1732

FRANCES TAYLOR
1700-1761

ELEANOR ROSE "NELLY" CONWAY
1731-1829

JAMES MADISON SR.
1723-1801

INFANT SON

ELIZABETH
1725-1773

FRANCES
1726-1776

JOHN TODD
1764-1793

DOLLEY PAYNE
1768-1849

JAMES MADISON
1751-1836

11
Brothers and
Sisters

JOHN PAYNE TODD
1792-1852

WILLIAM TEMPLE TODD
b./d. 1793

SHAY COCHRANE

125

APPENDIX B

Surprising Facts about James and Dolley Madison

✦ James Madison signed his name with "Junior" until his father's death in 1801.

✦ Indiana and Louisiana were admitted to the Union during Madison's term as president.

✦ Madison was one of the founders of the American Colonization Society.

✦ Madison attended Princeton University (then the College of New Jersey).

✦ Donald Robertson was Madison's first tutor; Madison attended his school in King and Queen County for five years and would later say, "All that I have been in my life, I owe largely to that man."

✦ Madison was thirty-six when the Constitutional Convention convened; he later became known as the Father of the United States Constitution. His notes of the convention were not published until after his death and remain the single most important source of its proceedings.

✦ During Thomas Jefferson's administration, Madison served as secretary of state and helped negotiate the Louisiana Purchase.

✦ Madison was the first U.S. president in history to preside over a declared war.

JMU SPECIAL COLLECTIONS

✦ Jefferson and Madison were close friends throughout their adult lives. Madison served on the board of visitors at the University of Virginia and upon Jefferson's death, assumed the position of rector.

✦ Madison was one of eight Virginians (Washington, Jefferson, Madison, Monroe, W. H. Harrison, Tyler, Taylor, Wilson) to serve as president of the United States.

✦ When Madison died on June 28, 1836, he was considered to be the last of the founding fathers.

✦ Madison was one of the three authors of *The Federalist Papers.*

✦ Madison was the nation's smallest chief executive at five feet, four inches tall and approximately 100 pounds.

✦ Madison was one of only two future U.S. presidents to sign the Constitution (George Washington was the other).

✦ Madison was the first president to come under enemy fire while in office (Battle of Bladensburg).

✦ The jacket Madison wore during his first presidential inauguration was woven from wool from sheep raised at Montpelier.

✳ Both of Madison's vice presidents died while in office (George Clinton and Elbridge Gerry).

✳ Madison was the author of the Virginia Resolution in opposition to the Alien and Sedition Acts.

✳ *Marbury v. Madison,* establishing the principle of judicial review, is considered to be one of the most significant Supreme Court decisions in U.S. history.

✳ One of the buildings of the Library of Congress is named for James Madison.

✳ Madison never ventured outside the territory of the United States.

✳ Madison originally proposed the Twenty-Seventh Amendment to the United States Constitution in the First Congress in 1789; it was not ratified until 1992.

✳ Dolley Madison came from a family of Quakers. They left North Carolina after freeing their slaves and moved to Philadelphia.

✳ Dolley was married first to John Todd. They had two children. Both John Todd and one child (William Temple Todd) died in the yellow fever epidemic in Philadelphia in 1793.

✳ James Madison and Dolley married in 1794; Madison was 17 years older than Dolley, and they had no children together.

✳ Aaron Burr, a college classmate of Madison, introduced James and Dolley.

✳ Dolley Madison assumed the role of White House hostess during Thomas Jefferson's administration because the president's wife had died much earlier.

✳ During the burning of Washington, D.C., Dolley is credited with saving the famous Gilbert Stuart painting of George Washington from destruction. Paul Jennings, one of Madison's slaves, states in his brief account published in 1865 that the portrait was actually rescued by the doorkeeper and gardener.

✳ Dolley Madison was the first former "first lady" to be photographed; a

LIBRARY OF CONGRESS

daguerreotype of her was made in 1848, just one year before her death.

✳ After James Madison's death, Dolley was forced to sell Montpelier (in 1844) to pay for the gambling debts of her only surviving son, Payne Todd.

✳ The term "first lady" was first used in reference to Dolley Madison, but was done so only after her death in her eulogy by President Zachary Taylor.

✳ Dolley was interred for eight years in the public and Causten vaults at Congressional Cemetery before her remains could be returned to Montpelier.

✳ Dolley Madison became a fashion setter for the nation's capital. One contemporary recorded, "She looked a Queen ... It would be *absolutely impossible* for any one to behave with more perfect propriety than she did."

Dolley Madison: First Lady and Widow of the Republic

She is a young lady of fourscore years and upward, goes to parties and receives company like the 'Queen of this New World.' — PHILIP HONE

JUST A FEW DAYS AFTER she had buried her husband and "beloved companion" in the family cemetery at Montpelier , Dolley Madison confided in a letter to her brother, "[I] have no power over my confused and oppressed mind to speak fully of the enduring goodness of my beloved husband. He left me many pledges of his confidence and love."1 The numerous expressions of sympathy and condolence that were arriving daily at Montpelier did, though, provide some comfort for her during this time of sorrow. They came from a variety of sources beginning with the faculty at the University of Virginia who wrote,

> *having this day learnt of the death of James Madison, former President of the United States, and late Rector of this institution, [the faculty] would not do justice to their feelings if they did not record their profound sense of his exalted worth—of those talents and public services which made him the pride & ornament of his Country, and of those mild virtues which proved an unfailing source of happiness to all around him.[2]*

Proclamations from the House of Representatives and United States Senate soon followed and on July 9, President Andrew Jackson wrote movingly to Dolley.

> *No expression of my own sensibility at the loss sustained by yourself and the Nation could add to the consolation to be derived from these high evidences of the Public sympathy. Be assured, Madam, that there is not one of your Countrymen who feels more poignantly the stroke which has fallen upon you, or who will cherish with a more endearing constancy the memory of the virtues, the services and the purity of the illustrious man whose glorious and patriotic life has been just terminated by a tranquil death.[3]*

Dolley's most immediate legal obligation was to execute the terms of her husband's will. Although she was the main beneficiary and inherited the Montpelier estate, Madison had left a variety of bequests that required time and energy to fulfill, including financial gifts of $2,000 to the American Colonization Society, $1,500 to the University of Virginia, and an additional $1,000 to his alma mater, Princeton.[4] The former president had died with the improvident belief that all of his widow's monetary needs would be forever secure soon after she arranged for the sale of his many papers for publication. Dolley Madison had spent years assisting her husband in compiling and transcribing these precious, historic documents, which chronicled the history and philosophical beginnings of the American republic. Yet, despite their intrinsic value, Dolley was horrified when no private publishing house expressed an interest in obtaining the rights to these materials. She had to turn to the federal government for relief, but it took twelve years of sluggish and often painful negotiations before Congress appropriated the paltry sum of $35,000 to buy the Madison manuscripts. The meager amount did nothing to offset her impending fiscal calamity, since most of the funds had to be diverted to offset her son's drinking and gambling debts. The result was that Dolley Madison, the former first lady of the American republic and the nation's most prominent widow, was left poor and destitute. On August 8, 1844, she was finally forced to face the inevitable and sell Montpelier. The final loss of her beloved home and estate seemed unbearable. She wrote, "No one I think, can appreciate my feeling of grief and dismay at the necessity of transferring to another a beloved home."[5]

Dolley was able to find some personal solace by moving back permanently to Washington, D.C. There she was able to enjoy the active social and political scene while basking in her unofficial title as "America's Queen."[6] Without the company of her husband, Dolley seemed to prefer the activity of city to the more tranquil life of the rural Virginia piedmont. Washington was a more exciting place, where she "could see always ... my valued acquaintances of that city."[7]

The Dolley Madison House. Located at 1520 H Street in Washington, D.C., Dolley Madison lived here after her husband's death. The house was owned initially by her brother-in-law, Richard Cutts, and was located in close proximity to the White House. Despite her serious financial difficulties, Dolley remained actively involved in the capital's social scene and maintained her reputation as an elegant hostess.

Dolley Madison eventually took up residence at the home of her niece, Anna Cutts. Located on the northeast corner of Lafayette Square, the house was in close proximity to the White House and Washington's energetic social hierarchy. Her continuing precarious financial situation, though, caused her continual anguish and worry. She was reduced to accepting charity from family and friends and even from her former servant, Paul Jennings, who remembered that

> *Mrs. Madison was a remarkably fine woman. She was beloved by everybody in Washington, white and colored ... In the last days of her life, before Congress purchased her husband's papers, she was in a state of absolute poverty, and I think suffered for the necessaries of life. While I was a servant to Mr. [Daniel] Webster, he often sent me to her with a market-basket full of provisions, and told me whenever I saw anything in the house I thought [Mrs. Madison] was in need of, to take it to her. I often did this and occasionally gave her small sums from my own pocket though I had years before bought my freedom from her.[8]*

Although she was financially destitute, Dolley continued to maintain a busy social schedule. She was a widely sought-after guest at various official and private functions. Historian Catherine Allgor explains that Dolley's "engagements proved so numerous that she bought a congressional directory, using it as a ledger sheet in order to keep track of her visiting debts."[9]

She attended some of the era's most significant events, including the presidential inauguration of James Polk. She was an honored guest at the ceremonies for the laying of the cornerstone of the Washington Monument—the first official memorial in the nation's capital honoring a former president. In 1844, Dolley Madison became a minor footnote in scientific history by becoming the first person to send a private telegraph message.[10] That same year, the House of Representatives honored Dolley by granting her a permanent seat in the legislative body's chamber. She courteously accepted the tribute in recognition of the memory of her husband's great esteem. She wrote to the Congress, "I shall be ever proud to recollect it, as a token of the remembrance, collective and individually, of one who has gone before us."[11]

In the 1840s, the science of photography was in its infancy. One creative and ambitious practioner of the new art was Mathew Brady.[12] He had strategically established a

LIBRARY OF CONGRESS

Mathew Brady's 1848 daguerreotype of Dolley Madison. Dolley Madison was the first presidential wife to be photographed. She was now an elderly widow, although John Quincy Adams remarked, "the depredations of time are not so perceptible in her appearance as might have been expected." The historic image disappeared until 1956, when it was discovered in a barn in Allentown, Pennsylvania. It was eventually donated to the Library of Congress.

photographic studio in Washington, D.C., and would later do so in New York City as well. His first ambitious project called for him to create a historic chronicle of the most notable personages of the day using the newly perfected daguerreotype process. Thomas Ritchie, a noted newspaper editor, agreed to serve as an intermediary between Brady and Mrs. Madison. In a letter he wrote to her in 1848, Richie explained that Brady "is very desirous of daguerreotyping that face, which is so well known to so many of our countrymen." He further noted, "he cannot think his gallery complete without adding your face to his interesting collection."[13]

Dolley Madison agreed to be photographed, and Brady took several remarkable images of the elderly Mrs. Madison. Using individually chemically treated plates, since the process did not allow for mass reproduction, the resulting pictures are a remarkable series of artifacts. They portray the ever fashionable Dolley in her favorite black dress and characteristic white turban.

The burial record for the Causten Vault. Dolley Madison died in 1849 and her remains were temporarily stored in the Public Vault at Congressional Cemetery. In February 1852, they were removed to the private Causten Vault. They remained there until 1858, when her remains were finally interred at the family cemetery at Montpelier.

On July 12, 1849, Dolley Madison died at the home of her niece, Anna Cutts. She was 81 years old and had been a widow for thirteen years. William O. Stevens observed, "Mrs. Madison was a power until the day of her death—even in her poverty and old age."[14] Her final days were chronicled in a letter written by her best friend, Elizabeth Collins Lee, who recounted, "I was with her every day during her illness—Tho greatly prostrate from the first she lay quiet, with her eyes shut and when not disturbed by the frequent attacks of her disease appeard to suffer no pain and conscious when spoken to tho she spoke but very faintly."[15]

The death of the nation's most adored first lady made an impact on the political world in an unprecedented manner. In an effort to give Dolley's grieving friends, family, and admirers the opportunity to pay their last respects, her body was laid out at her Washington home for a few days before being removed to the nearby St. John's Episcopal Church for the final funeral service. The services were "the largest yet seen in the city" and were attended by President Zachary Taylor, the cabinet, members of Congress, the Supreme Court, and diplomatic core. At the conclusion of the ceremonies, her body was transported to Congressional Cemetery, where it was placed in temporary repose in the cemetery's public vault until final arrangements could be made for her burial at Montpelier. The cost for the committal was five dollars.[16]

In one final act of insensitivity, Dolley's son, Payne Todd, failed to honor his mother's final wish to be buried alongside her husband. This alcoholic, derelict of a son had never even erected a monument to his stepfather at the Montpelier cemetery, a fact duly noted in *Frank Leslie's Illustrated*. "[Madison's grave was] undistinguished by monument of any kind. Only tradition pointed out the mound of earth which marked the last rest-

PHILIP BIGLER

The Causten Vault at Congressional Cemetery as it appears today.

ing-place of the great statesman."[17] Dolley Madison was forced to lay in repose in what amounted to a storage crypt for the next 30 months. In a notable historical coincidence, after Zachary Taylor's sudden death in 1850, the president's remains would likewise be stored temporarily in the public vault at Congressional alongside those of Dolley's.

In January 1852, Payne Todd died and was subsequently interred at Congressional. Dolley's beloved niece, Anna, had since married and arranged for her aunt's body to be moved to an adjacent and more suitable vault that was owned by her father-in-law, James Causten.[18] There Dolley's body would remain until January 12, 1858, when the remains were moved "to Virginia."[19] Dolley Madison was finally buried at Montpelier alongside her husband, partners in death as they had been in life.

ENDNOTES

Epigraph: Philip Hone quoted in Arnett, *Mrs. James Madison*, 390.

[1] Dolley Payne Todd Madison to Richard Cutts, in Shulman, *The Dolley Madison Digital Edition*, http://rotunda.upress.virginia.edu/dmde/DPM0879 (accessed 2008-09-10).

[2] University of Virginia Faculty to Dolley Payne Todd Madison, 29 June 1836, in Shulman, *The Dolley Madison Digital Edition*, http://rotunda.upress.virginia.edu/dmde/DPM0055 (accessed 2008-09-10).

[3] Andew Jackson to Dolley Payne Todd Madison, in Shulman, *The Dolley Madison Digital Edition*, http://rotunda.upress.virginia.edu/dmde/DPM0886 (accessed 2008-09-10).

[4] James Madison's will is available at http://www.jamesmadisonmus.org/textpages/will.htm. The will arranged for Dolley to receive all of Montpelier's slaves. "I give and bequeath my ownership in the negroes and people of color held by me to be my dear wife, but it is my desire that none of them should be sold without his or her consent, or in case of their misbehavior, except that infant children may be sold with their parents who consent for them to be sold with him or her, and who consent to be sold."

[5] Dolley Madison to Henry Moncure, 12 August 1844, in Mattern and Shulman, *Selected Letters of Dolley Payne Madison*, 323.

[6] Catherine Allgor, *A Perfect Union*, 6.

[7] Dolley Madison quoted in Fogle, *Two Hundred Years*, 41.

[8] Paul Jennings quoted in Arnett, 371. A good deal of information about Paul Jennings is available through the National Trust for Historic Preservation and the Decatur House, including his "bill of sale" to Pollard Webb in 1847 and subsequent work agreement with Daniel Webster. See http://www.preservationnation.org.

[9] Allgor, 380.

[10] Ibid., 380.

[11] Dolley Madison quoted in Arnett, 347-378.

[12] Mathew Brady would gain renown during the American Civil War for his battlefield images. He is buried at Congressional Cemetery.

[13] Thomas Ritchie to Dolley Madison, 2 May 1848, in Mattern and Shulman, 388.

[14] William O. Stevens quoted in Arnett, 390.

[15] Elizabeth Collins Lee letter to Zaccheus Collins Lee, 1849, in Mattern, 390.

[16] The original burial records are archived at Congressional Cemetery.

[17] *Frank Leslie's Illustrated* 30 January 1858 available at: http://www.loc.gov.

[18] The records at Congressional Cemetery indicate that Dolley Madison's remains were moved to the Causten vault on 10 February 1852.

[19] L. Williams was paid one dollar for "removing the body of Mrs. Madison from Causten's vault to be carried to Virginia."

Payne Todd: Prodigal Son

Nothing that Payne Todd ever had anything to do with seems to be improved by his meddling ... {He was a} cranky character to the last. — JAMES H. CAUSTEN

IN 1794, JAMES MADISON WAS FORTY-THREE YEARS OLD when he married the young, vivacious, and recently widowed Dolley Payne Todd. He was already a diligent scholar and established statesman, and he quickly assumed the added role of devoted stepfather to his wife's surviving two-year-old son, Payne Todd. Although Todd was not Madison's biological progeny, both he and Dolley would always refer to Payne affectionately as "our son."[1] Madison provided him with all of the love and support that a father should. Despite this, Payne chose not to emulate his "Papa's" success, preferring instead to chart a course through a life of privilege with countless episodes of recklessness, debauchery, drunkenness, and fiscal irresponsibility.[2] Payne Todd would ultimately become the proverbial prodigal son who returned his parents' love and devotion with little more than perpetual debt and endless disappointment.

By the age of ten, Todd was already revealing glimpses of his growing rebellious and unruly disposition. Madison, who was then serving as secretary of state in the Jefferson administration, still set aside time to personally tutor and supervise his stepson's education; but Payne cared little for ephemeral academic pursuits and was far more interested in pulling childish pranks and loitering in the stables than in serious study.[3] A few years later, Madison finally accepted the fact that all of his attempts to lead Payne "in the path of the Student" had been an abject failure.[4] Hoping to salvage his son's future, Madison enrolled him at St. Mary's College in Baltimore in hopes that this experience would provide him with a sound education and some semblance of discipline so that he may one day "do honor to his guardians."[5]

After eight years at the prestigious boarding school, Payne Todd had failed to distinguish himself, although he was, in Dolley's words, "much admired and respected as you could wish." He was a handsome, rakish, and charming young man and had become something of an "American prince," an ironic development in an infant republic that spurned such notions of hereditary entitlement.[6] His behavior continued to be irresponsible and undisciplined. In 1813, James Madison, now as president, attempted to give Payne some direction in life by appointing him to serve as a representative with an American peace commission destined for Europe. Madison desperately hoped that by living abroad, Todd would finally learn to accept responsibility and would additionally benefit from his association with his distinguished fellow commissioner, John Quincy Adams. These wishes proved delusional since Payne spent most of his time frivolously gambling and traveling around the continent at his parents' expense. According to historian Ralph Ketcham, Payne Todd had become "a classic example of the young American, warned of by Franklin and Jefferson, who was so dazzled by the courtly graces of Europe that he became unfit for useful life in his own country." After just two years overseas, the only thing Payne had acquired was a debt in excess of $8,000.[7]

While Payne spent the next years of his life pursuing his reckless routine of gambling, drinking, and spending, his parents unintentionally enabled him by regularly paying off his creditors, hoping in vain for the day when their son would finally marry, settle down, and assume responsibility. James and Dolley Madison, however, reacted differently and independently to their son's relentless quest for self-destruction. Madison's top priority was to keep his stepson out of debtor's prison while protecting Dolley from the painful knowledge of his incessant indiscretions. Regardless of Madison's efforts to "ensure her tranquility by concealing from her the ruinous extravagance of her son," Dolley was painfully aware of her son's situation.[8] She dealt with her public embarrassment and personal grief by continuously writing letters to Payne urging him to reform his objectionable behavior. She privately comforted herself by routinely denying the severity of his problems and refusing to acknowledge that her only child was, in fact, fatally flawed. Todd frequently disappeared for weeks at a time, frequenting a remarkable variety of taverns and brothels, according to of historian Virginia Moore.

> *That Payne was not only drinking and gambling but also, even now, involved in sexual derelictions seems highly probable in the light of a fragmentary journal written, partly in code, some years later, detailing—amid a few aesthetic appreciations—self-abuse and concourse with loose women, black and white, and his study of a book on venereal diseases.*[9]

His carousing led his mother to worry about his health and well-being. Her letters to him were often sad and frequently poignant. In 1845, Dolley wrote, "What has been the matter with you and [where] have you been my beloved? It has been long since you wrote me, or acknowledged the receiving of one of my several letters." Another note began: "If you love me, my dear son, write to me." Dolley was often dismayed when irrefutable evidence of Payne's recklessness became apparent, sometimes in the form of a single letter from him written while in prison. On one such occasion, Dolley Madison grieved, "My pride–my sensibility & every feeling of my Soul is wounded."[10] After years of enduring Todd's excesses and abuse, James Madison seemed to be nearing his limit. In 1824, after retiring yet another debt incurred by his stepson, this time totaling a staggering $20,000, Madison wrote his most candid letter ever to Payne.

> *What shall I say to you? ... Weeks have passed without even a line ... Whatever the causes of [your long absence and debts,] you owe it to yourself*

as well as to us, to withhold them no longer ... You cannot be too quick in affording relief to [your mother's] present feelings.[11]

Regardless of his continuing frustrations, Madison continued to rescue Payne from the consequences of his actions until the former president died at Montpelier on June 28, 1836.

One year later, Payne Todd returned to Orange County, ostensibly to live near his mother, but in reality he used the opportunity to pillage Montpelier of its valuable artifacts. He resided nearby on his own 104-acre plot, which he had purchased nineteen years earlier. Coincidently, according to historian Virginia Moore, the site had been already titled "Toddsberth" or "Todd's Camp" after one of the members of the Knights of the Golden Horseshoe who had encamped in the area in 1716.[12]

Safely away from the immediate temptations of the city, Payne undertook a variety of economic schemes, including an unsuccessful silk worm-raising endeavor. His most ambitious business venture was an effort to quarry marble on his estate. Dolley, perhaps encouraged by Payne's new found initiative, boasted of his interest in "geology," but the stone at Toddsberth proved unsuitable and, once again, he failed in life. Still, Payne was as reckless and manipulative as ever. As Virginia Moore wrote, while Payne was securely ensconced at Toddsberth, he enjoyed "living easy, going off on sprees, and bringing friends home to Montpelier whenever he liked for dinner or the night, or longer."[13]

It wasn't long before Payne Todd discovered yet another extravagant way to squander money. He spent yet another small fortune on needless home improvements and property development. He built relentlessly at Toddsberth, but without any sense of style or aesthetic. There were several cottages on the estate and an eccentric structure that was described as "a large round, towerlike building called the ball room." Anna Cutts, Payne Todd's cousin, wrote, "We looked [at] those buildings with sadness, for ridiculous in the eyes of a stranger, they were built with Mr. Todd's quaint ideas." Likewise, when a company of Confederate soldiers encamped in the area during the Civil War, J.H. Chamberlayne observed sardonically, "Payne Todd spent all the property Mr. Madison owned & most that Mrs. Madison got from the Government. The marks of the poor spendthrift are still to be seen, walks that he began, never to finish, an attempted ice house turned into a stately pleasure dome, like Kubla Kahn's; quarries opened for marble which was not there."[14]

One of the most selfish and ungrateful acts of Payne Todd's life occurred shortly after his mother's death in Washington, D.C. Having been forced to sell off Montpelier because of her son's debts and irresponsibility, Dolley Madison spent the last years of her life dependent upon the benevolence of others. During this time, she resided with her niece, Anna Cutts, who selflessly took care of her aunt and became Dolley's closest friend, companion, and confidante.[15]

Shortly after Dolley's death on July 16, 1849, Payne discovered to his horror that his mother's final will and testament decreed that he share with his cousin, Anna, fully half of the $20,000 congressional appropriation that had been allocated to purchase the remaining papers of James Madison. He began a series of expensive and needless legal proceedings to contest the document in court claiming that he should have been designated sole heir.

Portrait of Payne Todd and his grave at Congressional Cemetery. Payne died in January 1852 in Washington, D.C. A notorious alcoholic, he continually squandered his family's wealth, leaving his mother, Dolley, virtually destitute.

METROPOLITAN MUSEUM OF ART

Despite all of the stress he had caused his mother and all of the money he had wasted over the years, this was a final act of ingratitude. The courts appropriately ruled against him.[16]

Todd's regular alcoholic binges took a physical and psychological toll. His existing journals are embarrassingly incoherent and reveal a seriously troubled mind; they include such entries as: "Drank whiskey all day" and "Getting inebriated somewhat to cure indisposition."[17] His pathetic, half-hearted efforts to stop drinking (forsaking alcohol for ice water) repeatedly failed, and Payne finally admitted, "I seem sick for the want of [alcoholic spirits]."[18] Just three years after his mother's death, Payne Todd was badly injured in a fall. He then developed typhoid fever and tried to recuperate in Washington, D.C., but his condition only worsened. On his deathbed, he reportedly confided to a clergyman, "I forgive my enemies if I have any. I have never willfully injured anyone—but myself— I have been my own worst enemy."[19]

Payne Todd died on January 16, 1852, at the age of fifty-nine. He was buried the following day at Congressional Cemetery on "a stormy, snowy day, perhaps the very worst day of this hard winter," according to James Causten. He continues, "The few persons who attended were mostly his administrators and some of his past-companions and a few gentlemen who out of respect for his mother paid the last duty to his remains."[20] The newspapers charitably remembered him as the "late eccentric son of Mrs. Madison" who had a "strange and absorbing influence over his mother."[21] His funeral expenses totaled fifty-eight dollars.

ENDNOTES

Epigraph: James Causten quoted in Ethel Stephens Arnett, *Mrs. James Madison: The Incomparable Dolley* (Greensboro: Piedmont Press, 1972), 400.

[1] James Madison letter to Dolley Madison, ca. November 2, 1805, in Catherine Allgor *(A Perfect Union: Dolley Madison and the Creation of the American Nation* (New York: Henry Holt and Company, 2003), 112.

[2] Dolley often referred to James as Payne's "Papa" in her correspondence with Payne. For example, see Dolley Madison letter to Payne Todd December 2, 1824, in Virginia Moore, *The Madisons: A Biography* (New York: McGraw-Hill Book Company, (1979), 402.

[3] Moore, 164.

[4] Madison to Dolley Madison, November 19-20, 1805, Ibid.

[5] Dolley Madison to James Madison, November 2, 1805, in Allgor, 112.

[6] Ralph Ketcham, ed., *Selected Writings of James Madison* (Indianapolis: Hackett Publishing Company, 2006), 552.

[7] Ketcham, *Selected Writings,* 601.

[8] Madison to Edward Coles, February 23, 1827 in Allgor, 351.

[9] Moore, 415.

[10] Dolley Madison to Anna Payne Cutts June 6, 1829, quoted in Allgor, 352.

[11] James Madison to Payne Todd, 1825, in Ketcham, *Selected Writings,* 615.

[12] Moore, 379.

[13] Moore, 471.

[14] Matthew G. Hyland, *Montpelier and the Madisons: House, Home and American Heritage* (Charleston: The History Press, 2007), 93.

[15] Arnett, 390.

[16] Allgor, 401.

[17] Payne Todd quoted in Arnett, 362.

[18] Ibid., 362.

[19] Payne Todd quoted in Ketcham, *Selected Writings,* 616.

[20] James Causten quoted in Arnett, 400. There are no biographies of Payne Todd; he remains an extremely elusive and, in many ways, an unfathomable figure. His grave at Congressional Cemetery in Washington, D.C., is rarely visited, while his home, Toddsberth, in Orange County, Virginia, has virtually disappeared. There are no existing buildings from Todd's era to serve as his testament. Instead a modern chicken house stands on the site while nearby is the scarred earth from Todd's unsuccessful marble quarry, a silent reminder of Payne Todd's business folly. Information about Payne Todd's interment at Congressional Cemetery is available in Ethel Arnett's book, *Mrs. James Madison: The Incomparable Dolley.* This volume also contains some excellent primary resource materials, including several diary entries from James Causten. Her book also contains the most thorough account of Payne Todd available.

[21] *Fredericksburg News,* November 22, 1855.

The Deaths of James and Dolley Madison

JAMES MADISON DIED AT MONTPELIER ON JUNE 28, 1836

The eulogy of Mr. Madison is written in every page of the history of his country; to whose service his whole life was devoted, and with every great event in whose annals his names stands conspicuously and enduringly identified ... What honors ... are there, by which we can do justice to a character which history will hold up to future ages as a model of public and private virtue, not surpassed by the brightest examples in ancient or modern times? Sir, there are none. — SENATOR WILLIAM CABELL RIVES

From the *Daily National Intelligencer*
FRIDAY, JULY 1, 1836
"JAMES MADISON is no more!

The last of the great lights of the Revolution, the brightest of those great minds, which like the pillar of fire of old, conducted the American Israel through the trials of the scarcely less important era following the Revolution, and gave to his country the repose, security, and happiness of a wise, regular, stable, and consolidated Government; this pure and beautiful and benign light has at last sunk below the horizon, and is quenched forever in this world. Glorious indeed has been its long course, and though no more to be seen, it has left radiance in the firmament at which his country will long gaze with admiration and gratitude.

For more than thirty years, the name of JAMES MADISON has, more than that of any other living man, been associated, in the mind of United America, with the principles and the fabric of our Government. He was the principal architect in its construction, if he did not lay its corner-stone. He lived to see it endure many trials, survive great dangers, and to promise endurance for ages.

He died on the morning of Tuesday, the 28th of June. He was born on the 16th of March, in the year 1751; and was, of course, when he died, the patriarchal age of more than eighty-five years.

His end, visibly approaching for some days before, was such as that of a good and great man ought to be. His facilities undimmed till his latest hours, he expired without a struggle, free from pain, free from regret, and from cause of reproach."

DOLLEY MADISON DIED IN WASHINGTON, D.C., ON JULY 12, 1849

She will never be forgotten, because she was truly our First Lady
for a half-century. — PRESIDENT ZACHARY TAYLOR

From the *Daily National Intelligencer*
SATURDAY, JULY 14, 1849

"It is with saddened hearts that we announce to our readers the decease of Mrs. Madison, Widow of James Madison, Ex-President of the United States. She died at her residence in this city on Thursday night last, the 12th instant, between 10 and 11 o'clock, aged about eighty-two.

Beloved by all who personally knew her, and universally respected, this venerable Lady closed her long and well-spent life with the calm resignation which goodness of heart combined with piety only can impart. It would seem an abuse of terms to say that we regret the departure of one so ripe and so fitted for a better world. But, in the case of this excellent Lady, she continued until within a few weeks to grace society with her presence, and lend to it those charms with which she adorned the circles of the highest, the wisest, and best, during the bright career of her illustrious husband. Wherever she appeared, every one became conscious of the presence of the spirit of benignity and gentleness, united to all the attributes of feminine loveliness. For ourselves whose privilege it was to know and admire her through the last forty years of her life, it would not be easy to speak in terms of exaggeration of the virtues and winning manners of this eminent Lady. To attempt it would add no brightness to her fair name, and would be little needed to move the public sympathy. All of our own country and thousands in [distant] lands will need no language of Eulogy to inspire a deep and sincere regret when they learn the demise of one who touched all hearts by her goodness and won the admiration of all by the charms of dignity and grace."

TUESDAY, JULY 17, 1849
FUNERAL OF THE LATE MRS. MADISON

"The remains of the venerable relict of Ex-President Madison were removed from her late residence, in Lafayette square, to St. John's Church yesterday afternoon at 4 o'clock. The Rev. Mr. Pyne, Rector of the Church, delivered, in very feeling manner, an eloquent and just eulogy on the character of the deceased which was listened to with deep interest by a dense congregation including the President of the United States, the Cabinet Officers, gentlemen of the Army and Navy, the Mayor and City Councils, and many

St. John's Church. Dolley Madison's funeral service was held at St. John's Church on Lafayette Square. Her funeral was widely attended by the elite of Washington society, including the president, his cabinet, and the diplomatic core.

distinguished citizens and strangers. The Rev. Mr. French aided the Rector of St. John's in the funeral solemnities. About half past 5 o'clock the funeral procession, a very large and imposing one, moved from the Church to the Congress Cemetery, where the corpse will remain until it is removed to its final resting place at Montpelier, (Va.)."

From *Frank Leslie's Illustrated*
JANUARY 30, 1858

MONUMENT TO PRESIDENT MADISON

"Since his death and burial in 1836, the mortal remains of Ex-President Madison have been quietly reposing at Montpelier, in Orange county, Virginia, undistinguished by monument of any kind. Only tradition pointed out the mound of earth which marked the last resting-place of the great statesman. Several attempts to raise the necessary funds for a suitable monument to his memory failed, until some patriotic gentlemen of the vicinity, some months since, liberally advanced the money, and caused to be erected, on the 15th ult., at Montpelier, a structure which possesses all of the elements of strength, dignity and permanence.

The monument is constructed of James River granite. It is in form a simple obelisk. It is put together in seven pieces of massive stone, one of which is thirteen feet long, and another five feet by seven, weighing nine thousand pounds. The obelisk is twenty-two feet and six inches high, and weights thirty-two thousand pounds. The foundation being raised, the whole structure attains an elevation of twenty-four feet above the burying ground. About nine feet from the base is chiseled this simple inscription:

MADISON
Born March 16, 1751
Died June 28, 1836.

The appearance of the work will please every beholder. It is simple,

LIBRARY OF CONGRESS

James Madison's monument at Montpelier. Madison's grave remained unmarked for years, until finally a granite obelisk was erected. Frank Leslie's *Illustrated* reported that it was done after funds for the memorial were raised by "patriotic gentlemen of the vicinity."

Madison's burial vault. When erecting Madison's memorial marker, the vault containing his casket was exposed. The president had been dead 21 years.

substantial and graceful, and in strict keeping with the quiet of the country burial-place, and the modest but great character of the man whose grave it marks. A more pretentious pile would have been out of character with the man, and the retired, unfrequented place of his birth and death. All that was desirable was a structure to point out the place where his remains are to repose forever...

In digging for a suitable foundation, it became necessary to go below the coffin, which was consequently exposed to view. The boards placed above the coffin had decayed, but no earth had fallen in upon it, and everything appeared to be as when the coffin was deposited there, except that the coffin-lid was slightly out of place, allowing a partial view of the interior. As there were no fastenings to prevent, the part of the lid covering the superior portion of the body was raised, and several gentlemen present looked in upon the remains of the great Virginian. The coffin itself, of black walnut, was in perfect preservation, and the interior was nearly filled with a species of moss, which adhered pertinaciously to the wood. Beneath this, and partially hidden by it, were a few of the larger and harder bones. The lower jaw had fallen away, the bones of the breast and the ribs were gone, and the only parts of the skeleton which remained were the skull and portions of the cheek bones, the vertebrae of the neck, the spine and the large bones of the arms. All else of the upper part of the body had returned to the dust from whence it was taken, and in a few years more every trace of the body will disappear, until the trump of resurrection shall reunite the scattered particles. The body had been interred just twenty-one years."

ENDNOTES

Epigraph 1: Senator William Cabell Rives, speech on the Senate Floor, July 1836.

Epigraph 2: President Zachary Taylor's eulogy of Dolley Madison quoted in Hillary Clinton's speech on the unveiling of the Dolley Madison silver dollar in 1999. Available at http://clinton4.nara.gov/textonly/WH/EOP/First_Lady/html/generalspeeches/1999/19990111.html

Montpelier Resurrected

His house stands upon the Southwest Mountains, as they are called—a range of hills parallel to the Blue Ridge, and about twenty miles removed from it. There is a portico to it of the plainest and most massive order of architecture, but which Palladio gives as a specimen of the Tuscan. Mr. Madison himself superintended the building which he had executed by the hands of common workmen to whom he prescribed the proportions to be observed. It is of brick which requires and is intended to be plastered. — SIR AUGUSTUS FOSTER

FOR THE VAST MAJORITY OF VISITORS TO WASHINGTON, D.C., a day's pilgrimage to Thomas Jefferson's mountaintop home, Monticello, is essential. Thousands of tourists regularly drive the short two hours from the nation's capital down U.S. 29 to Charlottesville, but, until recently, only a few were willing to make the slight detour onto Route 290 to visit the ancestral home of James Madison. For those who did venture to Orange County, they were surprised when confronted with a massive, 55-room Victorian-era mansion. The house was a major dis-

appointment, in part because it was in a notable state of disrepair, and its brick façade was covered with a startling pink stucco. Horse tracks, Sears Catalog barns, and a one-lane bowling alley had dramatically altered the plantation's grounds, cluttering what one of Madison's visitors had described as, "successions of landscapes [which] varied at every turn, from the wildest to the most cultivated ... immense waving fields of grain, tobacco &c. in sight, the mountains cultivated, tho' so many miles distant."[1]

The original Madison mansion was constructed in the early 1760s

PHILIP BIGLER

The unrestored rear colonnade at Montpelier. After Madison's death in 1836, the house changed ownership several times. In the 1850s, the brick exterior was covered with a pink stucco.

PHILIP BIGLER

A Madison-era fireplace mantle undergoing restoration. Marion Scott duPont inherited Montpelier, which had been expanded into a massive mansion with fifty-five rooms. Many of the original Madison doors and fireplace mantles were reused during the expansion and eventually returned to their original locations.

and would undergo expansion and modification during James and Dolley Madison's lifetime.[2] After the president's death in 1836, Dolley inherited the entire estate, but she was financially unable to maintain it, hindered in part by the overwhelming gambling debts incurred by her alcoholic son, Payne Todd, and his inept management of her financial affairs. In 1844, Mrs. Madison reluctantly sold the Montpelier estate to a wealthy Richmond merchant, Henry W. Moncure. During the transaction, she plaintively wrote to him asking "that I should be permitted to choose some few, of the Negroes, and some of the furniture—and to retain the family Burial Place."[3] The house was destined to change ownership several times over the ensuing decades, with each owner freely altering, modifying, and modernizing the home to meet individual needs and desires.[4] Apparently, the infamous pink stucco was first applied by one of these subsequent owners during the 1850s.

In 1901, Montpelier was purchased by the millionaire businessman, William duPont. Under his stewardship, the Madison house was radically enlarged and expanded with a private train depot constructed for convenience along with a small general store. The grounds were likewise reconfigured to accommodate the duPonts' passion for American horse culture. In 1928, William duPont's daughter, Marion, established the Montpelier races. She would become renowned for her high quality thoroughbreds, which were often bred and raised at Montpelier. The most famous of her horses was Battleship, the sire of the legendary Man o' War, and the winner of the American Grand National and English Grand National steeplechases. After his death in 1958, the horse was buried at a prominent location near the original Madison ice house, alongside two of Mrs. duPont's other favorite horses, Annapolis and Accura.[5]

Marion Scott duPont was the last private owner of Montpelier. She died in 1983 and bequeathed the estate to the National Trust for Historic Preservation. In her will, she indicated her preference that the property be restored to honor James and Dolley Madison in "such manner as to conform as nearly as possible with the architectural pattern which existed when said property was owned and occupied by President Madison."[6]

Although much historical research was conducted on site to determine the architectural integrity of the house, it was not until 2001, when a grant from the Save America's Treasures program funded the first serious effort to restore the home to its antebellum appearance. Augmented by additional funding from the National Trust for Historic Preservation and the Mel-

The restored Montpelier. On Constitution Day 2008, the restored Montpelier was opened to the public. It appears today as it did during Madison's lifetime and now serves as a fitting memorial to the Father of the Constitution.

lon Foundation, extensive preservation efforts discovered that much of the original woodwork, fireplace mantles, doors, and windows had been recycled by the duPonts during their earlier expansions and that these Madison-era artifacts could be returned to their original locations. One of the most important archaeological finds was the discovery of a small mouse nest inside one of the mansion's interior walls. When removed and analyzed, it was discovered that the mouse had fortuitously nibbled off some of the Madisons' original wallpaper and in so doing, had preserved it for posterity. Also discovered in this valuable mouse nest were a scrap of a Fredericksburg newspaper and a fragment of a letter written in Madison's hand.

Effectively returning Montpelier to Madison's original design would require the destruction of most of the duPont's modern additions. According to the History Channel, "Restorers then tore down two wings, dismantled 14 bathrooms, rebuilt two staircases, and overall reduced the size of the mansion by more than half."[7] The entire process took seven years to complete, and the restored and resurrected Montpelier was unveiled to the public on Constitution Day 2008, a fitting memorial to the Father of the Constitution.

ENDNOTES

Epigraph: Augustus Foster quoted in Peterson, *Biography in His Own Words,* 214-215.

[1] Anna Thornton quoted in Mattern and Shulman, 20.

[2] The first major renovations came in 1797, when the house was converted into a duplex to accommodate both Dolley and James as well as his parents. The second expansion occurred from 1808 through 1812, with the addition of wings to the mansion and the construction of a rear colonade. Hillary Back, *The Restoration of Montpelier,* Harrisonburg, Va.: James Madison University, 2008), 3.

[3] Dolley Madison to Henry W. Moncure, September 3, 1844, in Mattern and Shulman, 376.

[4] Green, Miller and Hunt, 31.

[5] Information about the Montpelier Hunt Races and information about the estate's horse racing history is available at http://www.montpelierraces.com/history.html.

[6] Back, 4.

[7] Brad Spychalski, "James Madison's Montpelier Restored," *The History Channel Magazine* 7, (2009): 36.

APPENDIX G

The Quotable Mr. Madison

James Madison

❋ *We hold it for a fundamental and undeniable truth, that religion or the duty which we owe to our Creator and the manner of discharging it, can be directed only by reason and conviction, not by force or violence.*

MEMORIAL AND REMONSTRANCE, 1785

❋ *All men having power ought to be distrusted to a certain degree.*

JULY 11, 1787

❋ *We may define a republic to be … a government which derives all its powers directly or indirectly from the great body of the people, and is administered by persons holding their offices during pleasure, for a limited period, or during good behavior.*

THE FEDERALIST NO. 39

❋ *But what is government itself, but the greatest of all reflections on human nature? If men were angels, no government would be necessary.*

THE FEDERALIST NO. 51

❋ *In framing a government, which is to be administered by men over men, the great difficulty lies in this: you must first enable the government to control the governed, and in the next place, oblige it to control itself.*

THE FEDERALIST NO. 51

❋ *It will be of little avail to the people that the laws are made by men of their own choice, if the laws be so voluminous that they cannot be read, or so incoherent that they cannot be understood; if they be repealed or revised before they are promulged, or undergo such incessant changes that no man who knows what the law is today can guess what it will be to-morrow.*

THE FEDERALIST NO. 62

❋ *Governments destitute of energy, will ever produce anarchy.*

1788

✦ *Wherever the real power in a Government lies, there is the danger of oppression. In our Governments the real power lies in the majority of the community, and the invasion of private rights is chiefly to be apprehended, not from acts of Government contrary to the sense of its constituents, but from acts in which the Government is the mere instrument of the major number of the Constituents.*

LETTER TO THOMAS JEFFERSON, 1788

✦ *Since the general civilization of mankind, I believe there are more instances of the abridgment of freedoms of the people by gradual and silent encroachment of those in power than by violent and sudden usurpations.*

JUNE 6, 1788

✦ *It may be thought all paper barriers against the power of the community are too weak to be worthy of attention...Yet, as they have a tendency to impress some degree of respect for them, to establish the public opinion in their favor, and rouse the attention of the whole community, it may be one mean to controul the majority from those acts to which they might be otherwise inclined.*

JUNE 8, 1789

✦ *Of all the enemies to public liberty war, is, perhaps, the most to be dreaded.*

APRIL 20, 1795

✦ *Whilst it is universally admitted that a well-instructed people alone can be permanently a free people, and whilst it is evident that the means of diffusing and improving useful knowledge form so small a proportion of the expenditures for national purposes, I can not presume it to be unseasonable to invite your attention to the advantages of superadding to the means of education provided by the several States a seminary of learning instituted by the National Legislature within the limits of their exclusive jurisdiction, the expense of which might be defrayed or reimbursed out of the vacant grounds which have accrued to the nation within those limits.*

1810 STATE OF THE UNION ADDRESS

✦ *A silly reason from a wise man is never the true one.*

LETTER TO RICHARD RUSH, JUNE 27, 1817

✦ *If slavery, as a national evil, is to be abolished, and it be just that it be done at the national expense, the amount of the expense is not a paramount consideration.*

LETTER TO ROBERT J. EVANS, JUNE 15, 1819

✦ *A popular Government, without popular information, or the means of acquiring it, is but a prologue to a farce or a tragedy; or, perhaps, both. Knowledge will forever govern ignorance; and a people who mean to be their own governors must arm themselves with the power which knowledge gives.*

LETTER TO W. T. BARRY, AUGUST 4, 1822

✤ *Learned institutions ought to be favorite objects with every free people. They throw that light over the public mind which is the best security against crafty and dangerous encroachments on the public liberty.*

LETTER TO W. T. BARRY, AUGUST 4, 1822

✤ *Liberty and Learning; both best supported when leaning each on the other.*

LETTER TO W. T. BARRY, AUGUST 4, 1822

✤ *The magnitude of this evil [slavery] among us is so deeply felt, and so universally acknowledged; that no merit could be greater than that of devising a satisfactory remedy for it.*

1825

✤ *The best service that can be rendered to a Country, next to that of giving it liberty, is in diffusing the mental improvement equally essential to the preservation, and the enjoyment of the blessing.*

1826

✤ *The free system of government we have established is so congenial with reason, with common sense, and with a universal feeling, that it must produce approbation and a desire of imitation, as avenues may be found for truth to the knowledge of nations.*

LETTER TO PIERRE E. DUPONCEAU, JANUARY 23, 1826

✤ *The essence of Government is power; and power, lodged as it must be in human hands, will ever be liable to abuse.*

DECEMBER 2, 1829

✤ *The Constitution of the United States may doubtless disclose from time to time, faults which call for the pruning or the ingrafting hand. But remedies ought to be applied, not in the paroxysms of party and popular excitements; but with the more leisure and reflection … changes hastily accommodated to these vicissitudes would destroy the symmetry and the stability aimed at in our political system.*

LETTER TO JOHN M. PATTON, MARCH 24, 1834

✤ *As this advice, if it ever see the light, will not do so till I am no more, it may be considered as issuing from the tomb, where truth alone can be respected, and the happiness of man alone consulted. It will be entitled, therefore, to whatever weight can be derived from good intentions, and from the experience of one who has served his Country in various stations through a period of forty years; who espoused in his youth, and adhered through his life, to the cause of its liberty; and who has borne a part in most of the great transactions which will constitute epochs of its destiny. The advice nearest to my heart and deepest in my convictions is, THAT THE UNION OF THE STATES BE CHERISHED AND PERPETUATED.*

ADVICE TO MY COUNTRY 1834

James Madison University

Such a name would not only honor one of Virginia's greatest statesmen but an early champion of both public schools and higher education. Madison had realized the value of teacher training and had been a pioneer advocate of higher education for women. — RAYMOND C. DINGLEDINE JR.

THE STUDENTS OF JAMES MADISON UNIVERSITY show a special affection for the diminutive man they pass daily on their way to class. They loan him scarves in cold weather and give him cupcakes, necklaces and baseball caps. He is the go-to guy at every commencement, when graduates crowd into the flowerbed beside him to have their pictures taken.

"Jemmy" is the first of two statues of James Madison, Father of the Constitution, on the campus of the only American university to bear his name.[1] Its presence among contemporary students is a reminder that President James Madison's legacy remains essential and relevant. In addition to "Jemmy," another statue, this one heroic-sized and known as "Big Jim," was dedicated in 2008.

Founded in 1908 as the State Normal and Industrial School for Women at Harrisonburg in the Shenandoah Valley of Virginia, the school became the State Teachers College at Harrisonburg in 1924. Within a decade, it had become the largest women's teachers college in Virginia and a full liberal arts college. In 1938, it became Madison College, a name chosen by college President Samuel Duke. Extraordinary growth in the 1970s under the direction of President Ronald E. Carrier made a change to university status the next natural step. Madison College became James Madison University in 1977. In adopting Madison's name, the institution embraced one of the staunchest early advocates of public education, one who believed that education was essential to the animation of the principles of successful government.

The James Madison statue. Donated to JMU by Bruce and Lois Forbes, "Jemmy" has become a cherished campus icon.

Today James Madison University is a comprehensive university that is part of the statewide system of public higher education in Virginia. With an enrollment approaching 18,000, JMU offers programs on the bachelor's, master's and doctoral levels, with its primary emphasis on the undergraduate student.

JAMES MADISON UNIVERSITY

JMU continues to take inspiration from Madison, who wrote that a self-governing people "must arm themselves with the power which knowledge gives." The JMU community puts Madison's ideal of an enlightened citizenry to work in scholarship, research, outreach and public service. Professors and students collaborate across disciplines and engage with society beyond campus to address the big issues that affect the well being of humanity and the world.

Madison College acquired its name under President Samuel Duke. It became James Madison University in 1977 and has grown into a comprehensive university recognized nationally for its educational value and as an engaged campus.

To this end, JMU President Linwood H. Rose announced the opening of the James Madison Center opened in 1999 as a locus of outreach and study centering on the life of James Madison and the Federalist period. It is an important resource for teachers, students, and historians in teaching and promoting James Madison's legacy.

From its formative days as a teachers college, JMU has valued the critical role of faculty member as mentor, something President Madison benefited from as a student and expressly treasured long afterward. The mentor philosophy is embodied in the Donald Robertson Project, named in honor of James Madison's early tutor. Under the auspices of the James Madison Center, the project collaborates with K-12 educators, students, and communities. Through seminars, curricular materials, workshops, internships, and other platforms, the Donald Robertson Project invigorates Madison's ideal of the teacher as mentor.

In 2004, Congress passed legislation to establish an official federal holiday to celebrate the nation's founding document. The legislation set aside September 17, the date of the 1787 signing of the Constitution. West Virginia Senator Robert Byrd, the legislation's sponsor, said, "It seems obvious that a great republic cannot sustain itself unless its citizens participate in their own government. But how can they participate meaningfully if they don't know the fundamental principles on which their government is founded?"[2]

Far more than a simple affirmation of the anniversary, the bill required that the day be devoted to study of the Constitution. James Madison University had already long recognized the day. The 1787 Society, sponsored by the James Madison Center, is a student group dedicated to studying and practicing the ideals of James Madison. Open to students in all majors who meet the prerequisite grade-point average and qualifications, members help promote Madison's legacy to the student body, serve in an advisory capacity to the James Madison Center, and participate in two significant annual events, Constitution Day and James Madison Day.

James Madison University annually celebrates James Madison Day as part of a week-long observance of the man and his legacy, as well as the university's founding on March 14, 1908, a date of fortuitous coincidence with Madison's birth on March 16, 1751.

The university also maintains a strong relationship with Montpelier, the plantation of James Madison, located some fifty miles east of the campus in Orange County, Virginia. In 1986, archaeology professor Clarence Geier initiated the JMU-Montpelier archaeology field school. Students began the painstaking and historically significant work of unearthing the history of Madison's estate and the earlier Mount Pleasant homestead. Working closely with Montpelier's archaeologists over the years, JMU students and professors have helped uncover some of Montpelier's secrets and have assisted the restorers in returning the house to Madison's era. The restored Montpelier opened its doors to the public the same year, 2008, that the university celebrated its own centennial, another notable coincidence.

In 1999, JMU finalized a formal partnership agreement with Montpelier to provide collaborative programs of education and outreach beyond archaeology. The next year, students conducted architectural, archaeological, and historical research, including oral histories of descendants, pertaining to a mid-nineteenth-century cabin once occupied by the emancipated African-American slave, George Gilmore.

JAMES MADISON UNIVERSITY

Students enjoy an early spring on the Quad at JMU, the only institution of higher education named for James Madison.

James Madison's intellectual and civic example is alive and well at James Madison University today. Regularly ranked nationally as a top university, a best value and an engaged campus,[3] JMU offers the wide array of opportunities associated with a large research university with the atmosphere of a small liberal arts college. JMU offers 106 degree programs, including sixty-eight on the undergraduate level, thirty master's, two educational specialist, and six doctoral. Programs include integrated science and technology, the sustainability-focused School of Engineering, as well as powerful programs in the traditional sciences. Recognized for the high quality of its undergraduate research opportunities in the sciences and humanities and a top-rated College of Business, JMU is also known for the quality of its teacher education, fine and performing arts, community service-learning, and its heavy emphasis on Study Abroad and international experiences. The energy of this large campus finds a cohesion of purpose in a powerfully simple mission statement:

We are a community committed to preparing students to be educated and enlightened citizens who lead productive and meaningful lives.

Unlike Thomas Jefferson, Madison's close friend, who participated in the construction of his University of Virginia, President Madison never saw James Madison University. But that would have mattered little to this man of ideas. The advancement of his political philosophy and his fidelity to the power of education and the importance of civil discourse probably would have pleased him far more than any building or monument. It is the daily work of educating the next generation that truly provides a living testament to the ongoing legacy of James Madison.

By MARTHA GRAHAM

ENDNOTES

Epigraph: Raymond C. Dingledine Jr., *Madison College: The First Fifty Years, 1908-1958,* (Harrisonburg, Va: Madison College, 1959), 222.

[1] James Madison College, in East Lansing, Michigan, is a division of Michigan State University.

[2] Robert Byrd quoted in Christopher Lee, "New Law Requires Workers to Learn About Constitution," *The Washington Post,* 20 July 2005, P. A21.

[3] A summary of JMU's rankings can be found at http://www.jmu.edu/jmuweb/aboutJMU/national_recognitions.shtml. They include, among others: fifteen years in a row as the top public master's level university in the South by *U.S. News and World Report*; a best value by *Kiplinger Personal Finance* magazine; and a "college with a conscience" by *The Princeton Review* and Campus Compact. The 2009 *Princeton Review* also recognized JMU as one of the nation's top 50 "Best Value" public universities; See http://www.jmu.edu/jmuweb/general/news/general10363.shtml).

SELECTED BIBLIOGRAPHY

Abbot, W. W., ed. *The Papers of George Washington: September 1788-March 1789*. Charlottesville: University Press of Virginia, 1987.

Adair, Douglass. "James Madison's Autobiography." *The William and Mary Quarterly* 2, no. 2 (April 1945): 191-209.

Allgor, Catherine. *A Perfect Union: Dolley Madison and the Creation of the American Nation*. New York: Henry Holt and Company, 2006.

Anderson, William Kyle. *Donald Robertson and his Wife Rachel*. Self-published manuscript, 1900.

Arkin, Marc M. "The Federalist Trope: Power and Passion in Abolitionist Rhetoric." *The Journal of American History* 88, no.1 (2001): 75-98.

Arnett, Ethel Stephens. *Mrs. James Madison: The Incomparable Dolley*. Greensboro: Piedmont Press, 1972.

Back, Hillary. *The Restoration of Montpelier*. Harrisonburg, Va.: James Madison University, 2008.

Bailyn, Bernard, ed. *The Debate on the Constitution: Federalists and Antifederalist Speeches during the Struggle over Ratification*. New York: Library of America, 1993.

Berkin, Carol. *A Brilliant Solution: Inventing the American Constitution*. New York: Harcourt, Inc., 2002.

Bernstein, Richard B., and Jerome Agel. *Amending America: If We Love the Constitution So Much, Why Do We Keep Trying to Change It?* New York: Time Books, 1993.

Bigler, Philip. *Washington in Focus: A Photo History of the Nation's Capital*. St. Petersburg, Fla.: Vandamere Press, 1994.

Billings, W. M., John Selby, and Thad W. Tate. *Colonial Virginia: A History*. New York: KTO Press, 1986.

Bork, Robert. *The Tempting of America: The Political Seduction of the Law*. New York: The Free Press, 1990.

Borneman, Walter R. *1812: The War that Forged A Nation*. New York: Harper Perennial, 2005.

Bowling, Kenneth R. and Helen E. Veit, eds. *The Diary of William Maclay and Other Notes on Senate Debates: March 4, 1789-March 3, 1791*. Baltimore: Johns Hopkins University Press, 1988.

Brant, Irving. *The Fourth President: A Life of James Madison*. Connecticut: Easton Press, 1970.

Brant, Irving. *James Madison, Father of the Constitution: 1787-1800*. Indianapolis: The Bobbs-Merrill Company, Inc., 1950.

Brant, Irving. *James Madison: The President 1809-1812*. Indianapolis: The Bobbs-Merrill Company, Inc., 1956.

Brant, Irving. "Madison: On the Separation of Church and State." *The William and Mary Quarterly* 8, no. 1 (January 1951): 3-24.

Brodie, Fawn M. "Thomas Jefferson's Unknown Grandchildren, October 1976." *American Heritage* http://www.americanheritage.com.

Brown, Richard D., ed. *Major Problems in the Era of the American Revolution: 1760-1791.* Major Problems in American History. New York: Houghton-Mifflin Company, 2000.

Brugger, Robert J., ed. *The Papers of James Madison: Secretary of State Series, 4 March 1801-31 July 1801.* Charlottesville, VA., University of Virginia Press, 1986.

Burns, Eric. *The Smoke of the Gods: A Social History of Tobacco.* Philadelphia: Temple University Press, 2007.

Carter, Bradley Kent and Joseph F. Kobylka. "The Dialogic Community: Education, Leadership, and Participation in James Madison's Thought." *The Review of Politics* 52, no. 1 (Winter 1990): 32-63.

Cerami, Charles. *Young Patriots: The Remarkable Story of Two Men, Their Impossible Plan and the Revolution that Created the Constitution.* Naperville, Ill.: Sourcebooks, Inc., 2005.

Chambers, Douglas B. *Murder at Montpelier: Igbo Africans in Virginia.* Jackson, Miss.: University Press of Mississippi, 2005.

Chapman, Charles Thomas. "Who Was Buried in James Madison's Grave? A Study in Contextual Analysis." Master's thesis, College of William and Mary, 2005.

Collier, Christopher and James Collier. *Decision in Philadelphia: The Constitutional Convention of 1787.* New York: Random House, 1986.

Crawford, Alan Pell. *Twilight at Monticello: The Final Years of Thomas Jefferson.* New York: Random House, 2008.

Cromwell, John W. "The Aftermath of Nat Turner's Insurrection." *The Journal of Negro History* 5, no. 2 (April 1920): 208-235.

Denison, Dave. "Happy Constitution Day! A New Law Requires Schools to Observe an Old Holiday in the Constitution's Honor. But is Constitution Day Constitutional?" *The Boston Globe,* September 18, 2005.

Dicken-Garcia, Hazel. *Journalistic Standards and the Press's Role to 1850.* Madison: University of Wisconsin Press, 1989.

Dillon, Sam. "From Yale to Cosmetology School, Americans Brush Up on History and Government." *New York Times,* 16 September 2005, A14.

Shulman, Holly C., ed. *The Dolley Madison Digital Edition.* Charlottesville: University of Virginia Press, 2004. http://rotunda.upress.virginia.edu.

Durey, Michael. *"With the Hammer of Truth": James Thomson Callender and America's Early National Heroes.* Charlottesville: University of Virginia Press, 1990.

Eastern Argus, (Portland, M.A.) 28 October 1831.

Ellis, Joseph. *American Creation: Triumphs and Tragedies at the Founding of the Republic.* New York: Alfred A. Knopf, 2007.

Ellis, Joseph. *Founding Brothers: The Revolutionary Generation*. New York: Alfred A. Knopf, 2001.

Ellis, Joseph. *His Excellency: George Washington*. New York: Vintage Books, 2004.

Farish, Hunter Dickenson, ed. *Journal and Letters of Philip Vickers Fithian: A Plantation Tutor of the Old Dominion, 1773-1774*. Charlottesville: University Press of Virginia, 1983.

Fogle, Jeanne. *Two Hundred Years: Stories of the Nation's Capital*. Alexandria, Va.: Vandamere Press, 1991.

Fox, Early Lee. *The American Colonization Society 1817-1840*. Baltimore: The Johns Hopkins Press, 1919.

Fredericksburg News. (Fredericksburg, Va.) 1855.

"Further Particulars of the Capture of Nat Turner." *Eastern Argus*, 15 November 1831, 1.

Glod, Maria. "Students Examine Who Has a Place in 'We the People'; Pondering U.S. Constitution Mandated on Its Anniversary." *Washington Post*, 17 September 2005.

Gray, Elizabeth S. "Donald Robertson and His School in King and Queen County." *The Bulletin of the King and Queen County Historical Society of Virginia*, 1963, 14: 2-6.

Green, Bryan Clark, Ann L. Miller and Conover Hunt. *Building a President's House: The Construction of James Madison's Montpelier*. Orange, Va.: The Montpelier Foundation, 2007.

Greene, Jack P., ed. *The Diary of Landon Carter of Sabine Hall, 1752-1778*. Charlottesville: The University Press of Virginia, 1965.

Greenberg, Kenneth S., ed. *The Confessions of Nat Turner and Related Documents*. The Bedford Series in History and Culture. Boston: Bedford Books of St. Martin's Press, 1996.

Hackett, Mary, ed. *The Papers of James Madison: Secretary of State Series, 1 September 1804-31 January 1805*. Charlottesville: University of Virginia Press, 2007.

Harper's Weekly, 6 February 1858.

Hyland, Matthew G. *Montpelier and the Madisons: House, Home and American Heritage*. Charleston: The History Press, 2007.

Hitchens, Christopher. *Thomas Jefferson: Author of America*. New York: HarperCollins, 2005.

Hogan, Pendleton. *The Lawn: A Guide to Jefferson's University*. Charlottesville: Rector and Board of Visitors, 1996.

Holmes, David. *Jefferson and Religion*. Ash Lawn, Va.: Monticello-Stratford Seminar, 2008.

Horton, Daniel. *Admiring Failures: An Examination of James Madison's Attitudes Towards Slavery and His Attempts to Eliminate It*. Harrisonburg, Va.: James Madison University, 2008.

Hunt, Gaillard, ed. *The Writings of James Madison, comprising his Public Papers and his Private Correspondence, including his numerous letters and documents now for the first time printed*. New York: G. P. Putnam's Sons, 1900.

Hutchinson, William T., ed. *The Papers of James Madison 16 March 1751-16 December 1779*. Chicago, Ill.: University of Chicago Press, 1962.

Hutchinson, William T. *The Papers of James Madison 3 May 1783-20 February 1784*. Chicago: University of Chicago Press, 1971.

Hyland, Matthew G. *Montpelier and the Madisons: House, Home and American Heritage* Charleston: The History Press, 2007.

Isaac, Rhys. *Landon Carter's Uneasy Kingdom: Revolution and Rebellion on a Virginia Plantation*. New York: Oxford University Press, 2004.

"James Madison's Montpelier." http://www.montpelier.org/explore/gardens/cemeteries_madison.php.

"Jefferson's Blood." *Frontline*. PBS Video, 1999.

Jennings, Paul. *A Colored Man's Reminiscences of James Madison*. Brooklyn: George C. Beale, 1865.

Jennings, L. Wagoner. "Honor and Dishonor at Mr. Jefferson's University: The Antebellum Years." *History of Education Quarterly* 26, no. 2 (Summer 1986): 155-179.

Johnson, Elizabeth C. "John Baylor, Master of New Market." *The Bulletin of the King and Queen Historical Society* 47 (1979): 4.

Ketcham, Ralph, ed. James Madison: A Biography. Charlottesville: The University Press of Virginia, 1990.

Ketcham, Ralph, ed. *Selected Writings of James Madison*. The American Heritage Series. Indianapolis: Hackett Publishing Company, Inc., 2006.

Ketcham, Ralph, ed. *Selected Writings of James Madison*. The American Heritage Series. Indianapolis: Hackett Publishing Company, Inc., 2006.

Koch, Adrienne. *Jefferson and Madison: The Great Collaboration*. New York: Oxford University Press, 1980.

Koch, Adrienne, ed. *Notes of Debates in the Federal Convention of 1787 Reported by James Madison*. Athens: Ohio University Press, 1984.

Kurland, Philip B. and Ralph Lerner, ed. *The Founder's Constitution*. Chicago: University of Chicago Press, 1987.

Labunski, Richard. *James Madison and the Struggle for the Bill of Rights*. New York: Oxford University Press, 2006.

Lambert, Frank. *The Founding Fathers and the Place of Religion in America*. Princeton: Princeton University Press, 2003.

Leibiger, Stuart. *Founding Friendship: George Washington, James Madison, and the Creation of the American Republic*. Charlottesville: University Press of Virginia, 1999.

Macon Weekly Telegraph, 10 September 1831.

Madison, James. "James Madison's Attitude toward the Negro." *The Journal of Negro History* 6, no. 1 (January 1921): 74-102.

Madison, James. The Federalist No. 10. http://thomas.loc.gov/home/histdox/fed_10.html.

Madison, James. The Federalist No. 51. http://thomas.loc.gov/home/histdox/fed_51.html.

Malone, Dumas. *Jefferson and His Time: The Sage of Monticello.* Boston: Little, Brown and Company, 1981.

Martineau, Harriet. *Retrospect of Western Travel.* Armonk, N.Y.: M.E. Sharpe, 2000.

Mattern, David B., ed. *James Madison's "Advice to My Country."* Charlottesville: The University Press of Virginia, 1997.

Mattern, David B., ed. *The Papers of James Madison, 31 March 1797-3 March 1801.* Charlottesville: The University Press of Virginia, 1991.

Mattern, David B. and Holly C. Shulman, eds. *The Selected Letters of Dolley Payne Madison.* Charlottesville: The University Press of Virginia, 2003.

Mayer, Henry. *A Son of Thunder: Patrick Henry and the American Revolution.* New York: Grove Press, 1991.

McCoy, Drew R. *The Last of the Fathers: James Madison & the Republican Legacy.* Cambridge: Cambridge University Press, 1998.

McCullough, David. *John Adams.* New York: Simon & Schuster, 2001.

McDonald, Robert. "The Madison Legacy: A Jeffersonian Perspective." *James Madison and the Future of Limited Government.* ed. John Samples. Washington, DC: Cato Institute, 2002.

Memoirs of Israel Jefferson http://www.pbs.org/wgbh/pages/frontline/shows/jefferson/cron/1873israel.html.

Meyers, Marvin, ed. *Sources of the Political Thought of James Madison.* Hanover: University Press of New England, 1981.

Miller, Ann L. Interview by Philip Bigler and Annie Lorsbach, 3 June 2008.

Miller, Ann L. *The Short Life and Strange Death of Ambrose Madison.* Orange, Va.: Orange County Historical Society, 2001.

Miller, William Lee. *The Business of Next May: James Madison and the Founding.* Charlottesville: The University Press of Virginia, 1992.

Moore, Virginia. *The Madisons: A Biography.* New York: McGraw-Hill Book Company, 1979.

Mosteller, Frederick. "A Statistical Study of the Writing Styles of the Authors of 'The Federalist' Papers." *Proceedings of the American Philosophical Society* 131, no. 2 (June 1987): 132-140.

Muñoz, Vincent Phillip. "James Madison's Principle of Religious Liberty." *The American Political Science Review* 97, no. 1 (February 2003): 17-32.

Neiman, Fraser D. "Coincidence or Casual Connection? The Relationship between Thomas Jefferson's Visits to Monticello and Sally Heming's Conceptions." *William and Mary Quarterly* 57, no. 1 (2000): 198-210.

Onuf, Peter. "Every Generation Is an 'Independent Nation': Colonization, Miscegenation, and the Fate of Jefferson's Children." *The William and Mary Quarterly* 57, no. 1 (January 2000): 153-170.

Pasley, Jeffrey L. *The Tyranny of Printers: Newspaper Politics in the Early American Republic.* Charlottesville: University Press of Virginia, 2001.

Peabody, James Bishop, ed. *John Adams, A Biography in His Own Words.* New York, Newsweek, 1977.

Peterson, Merrill D., ed. *The Founding Fathers James Madison: A Biography in His Own Words.* The Papers of James Madison. New York: Newsweek, 1974.

Rakove, Jack. *James Madison and the "Vices of the Political System of the United States:" A Constitution for the Ages: James Madison the Framer.* Lecture at Princeton University, 2001.

Rakove, Jack N., ed. *James Madison: Writings.* New York: The Library of America, 1999.

Richards, Leonard L. *Shay's Rebellion: The American Revolution's Final Battle.* Philadelphia: University of Pennsylvania Press, 2002.

Richmond Enquirer, 4 October 1831.

Rutland, Robert A., ed. *James Madison and the American Nation: An Encyclopedia.* New York: Charles Scribner's Sons, 1994.

Rutland, Robert A., ed. *The Papers of James Madison: 10 March 1784 - 28 March 1786.* Chicago: University of Chicago Press, 1973.

Rutland, Robert A., ed. *The Papers of James Madison: 9 April 1784 - 24 May 1787.* Chicago: University of Chicago Press, 1975.

Rutland, Robert A., ed. *The Papers of James Madison: 7 March 1788 - 1 March 1789.* Charlottesville: University Press of Virginia, 1977.

Salem Gazette, 6 September 1831.

Sentinel and Witness (Middletown, Conn.) 1831.

Slaughter, Philip. *The Virginian History of African Colonization.* Richmond: MacFarlane & Fergusson, 1855.

Smith, Abbot Emerson. *James Madison: Builder.* New York: Wilson-Erickson Inc., 1937.

Smith, James Morton, ed. *The Republic of Letters: the Correspondence between Thomas Jefferson and James Madison 1776-1826.* New York: W.W. Norton & Company, 1995.

Sorensen, Leni A. "Madison Hemings Naming," 5 March 2008, personal e-mail.

Spychalski, Brad. "James Madison's Montpelier Restored." *The History Channel Magazine*, 2009, 36.

Stagg, J. C. A., ed. *The Papers of James Madison: 27 April 1795-March 1797.* Charlottesville: University of Virginia Press, 1989.

Stagg, J. C. A., ed. *The Papers of James Madison: 5 November 1811-9 July 1812.* Presidential Series. Charlottesville: University Press of Virginia, 1999.

Staudenraus, P. J. *The African Colonization Movement: 1860-1865.* New York: Octagon Books, 1980.

Stewart, David O. *The Summer of 1787: The Men Who Invented the Constitution.* New York: Simon & Schuster, 2007.

Swaney, W. B. "Religious Freedom." *Virginia Law Review* 12, no. 8 (June 1926): 632-644.

Syrett, Harold C. and Jacob E. Cooke, ed. *The Papers of Alexander Hamilton: 1782-1786.* New York: Columbia University Press, 1962.

Syrett, Harold C. and Jacob E. Cooke, ed. *The Papers of Alexander Hamilton: 1787-May 1788.* New York: Columbia University Press, 1962.

Taylor, Beth. "James Madison and Slavery." Lecture at James Madison University, 2008.

The Washington Post, 20 July 2005.

The Washington Times, 25 September 2006.

Thorp, Willard. *The Lives of Eighteen from Princeton.* Princeton, N.J.: Princeton University Press, 1946.

Wagoner, Jennings. "Honor and Dishonor at Mr. Jefferson's University: The Antebellum Years." *History of Education Quarterly* 26, no. 2 (Summer 1986): 155-179.

Waldman, Steven. *Founding Faith: Providence, Politics, and the Birth of Religious Freedom in America.* New York: Random House, 2008.

Ward, Geoffrey C. *The Civil War: An Illustrated History.* New York: Alfred A. Knopf, 1990.

Weber, Paul J. "James Madison and Religious Equality: The Perfect Separation." *The Review of Politics* 44, no. 2 (April 1982): 163-186.

Webster, M. E., ed. *The Federalist Papers Modern English,* second edition, http://Mary.Webster.org., 2008.

Weisberger, Bernard A. *America Afire: Jefferson, Adams, and the Revolutionary Election of 1800.* New York: HarperCollins Publishers, 2000.

Wheelan, Joseph. *Jefferson's War: America's First War on Terror 1801-1805.* New York: Carroll & Graf Publishers, 2003.

Whitfield, Theodore M. *Slavery Agitation in Virginia: 1829-1832.* New York: Negro Universities Press, 1930.

Wilentz, Sean. *The Rise of American Democracy: The Crisis of the New Order: 1787-1815.* New York: W.W. Norton and Company, 2005.

Wilkins, Roger. *Jefferson's Pillow: The Founding Fathers and the Dilemma of Black Patriotism.* Boston: Beacon Press, 2002.

Wills, Garry. *James Madison.* New York: Time Books, 2002.

Wills, Garry. *Mr. Jefferson's University.* Washington, D.C.: National Geographic Society, 2002.

Wills, Garry. *Negro President: Jefferson and the Slave Power.* Boston: Houghton Mifflin Company, 2005.

Wright, J. Handly. "The Remarkable Scholars of Donald Robertson." *The Bulletin of the King and Queen Historical Society* 44 (1978): 5.

Yarema, Allan. *The American Colonization Society: An Avenue to Freedom.* Lanham, Md.: University Press of America, 2006.

PHOTOGRAPH AND ILLUSTRATION CREDITS

Washington Skyline, View from Arlington National Cemetery
Photograph by Philip Bigler

Rotunda at the National Archives
Courtesy of the National Archives

Fry-Jefferson Map of Virginia 1751
Courtesy of the National Archives

Madison Birthplace Historical Marker
Photograph by Philip Bigler

Original Painting of Mount Pleasant
Painting by Linda Boudreaux Montgomery

James Madison University Archaeology Student at Mount Pleasant
Courtesy of Matt Reeves
Director of Archaeology, Montpelier

Donald Robertson Account Book 1758-1775
Courtesy of Virginia Historical Society
Mss5:3 R5456:1

City of Philadelphia
Courtesy of the National Archives

Portrait of the Reverend John Witherspoon
Courtesy of Princeton University Archives
Department of Rare Books and Special Collections, Princeton University Library

The Lawn at the University of Virginia
Henry Schenck Tanner after a drawing by Benjamin Tanner. "Village Design of University of Virginia," 1826. Detail of *University of Virginia* map by Herman Böÿe, 1827. Reproduction courtesy of the Tracy W. McGregor Library of American History, Special Collections Department, University of Virginia Library (76)

Old Bruton Parish Church
Williamsburg, Virginia
Library of Congress,
Prints & Photographs Division
#LC-USZ62-15194

Great House at Stratford Plantation
Photograph by Philip Bigler

The Scarecrow
Painting by Allen Carter Redwood
Courtesy of Virginia Historical Society
2000.45

Portrait of George Mason
Painting by Louis Mathieu Didier Guillaume
Courtesy of Virginia Historical Society
1858.2

Assembly Room in Independence Hall
Courtesy of Independence National
Historical Park

United States Constitution
Courtesy of the National Archives

Rising Sun Chair and Detail (Composite)
Courtesy of Independence National
Historical Park

United States Constitution
Courtesy of the National Archives

Portrait of Patrick Henry
Library of Congress
Prints and Photographs Division
#LC-D429-29019

George Washington Delivering His Inaugural Address Before Members of the Congress
Library of Congress
Prints and Photographs Division
#LC-USZ62-2261

Federal Hall, Wall Street
Library of Congress
Prints and Photographs Division
#LC-USZ62-95064

Portrait of John Adams
Courtesy of the National Archives

Congressional Pugilists
Library of Congress
Prints & Photographs Division
#LC-USZ62-1551

Masthead of *Porcupine's Gazette*
Author's personal collection

The "Humane" British and
Their "Worthy" Allies
Library of Congress
Prints and Photographs Division
#LC-USZ62-5800

The Taking of the City of Washington
Library of Congress
Prints and Photographs Division
#LC-USZ62-1939

The Hartford Convention
Library of Congress
Prints and Photographs Division
#LC-USZ62-7831

Original Painting of Enslaved Community
South Yard
Painting by Linda Boudreaux Montgomery

Dinsmore's Drawing of Montpelier
Courtesy of Virginia Historical Society
Mss5:10 B5628:1

Census 1830
Courtesy of the National Archives

Jefferson's Farm Book
Farm Book, 1774-1824, page 128, by Thomas Jef-
ferson. Original manuscript from the Coolidge
Collection of Thomas Jefferson Manuscripts
Massachusetts Historical Society.

Horrid Massacre in Virginia
Library of Congress
Prints and Photographs Division
#LC-USZ62-38902

Original Painting of Slave Cemetery
Painting by Linda Boudreaux Montgomery

Menokin
Photograph by Philip Bigler

Battle of Antietam
Library of Congress
Prints and Photographs Division
#LC-B811-562

Union Must Be Preserved
Library of Congress
Prints and Photographs Division
#LC-USZ62-14861

Portrait of James Madison
Courtesy of James Madison University Library
Special Collections

Portrait of Dolley Madison
Library of Congress
Prints and Photographs Division
#LC-USZ62-68175

Dolley Madison House,
17 & H, Washington, D.C.
Library of Congress
Prints and Photographs Division
#LC-DIG-npcc-00129

Portrait of Dolley Madison,
half plate daguerreotype
Library of Congress
Prints and Photographs Division
#LC-USZ62-110198

Congressional Cemetery 1852 Burial Record
Photograph by Philip Bigler

Causten Vault
Photograph by Philip Bigler

Portrait of Payne Todd
Courtesy of The Metropolitan Museum of Art
Gift of Miss Mary Madison McGuire, 1936
Image ©The Metropolitan Museum of Art
36.73

St. John's Church
Library of Congress
Prints and Photographs Division
#LC-USZ62-56583

Madison Grave
Frank Leslie's Illustrated, January 30, 1858
Library of Congress
Prints and Photographs Division
#LC-USZ62-127063

Madison Vault
Frank Leslie's Illustrated, January 30, 1858
Library of Congress,
Prints and Photographs Division
#LC-USZ62-127063

Rear Colonnade of Montpelier
Photograph by Philip Bigler

Fireplace Mantelpiece at Montpelier
Photographer by Philip Bigler

Restored Montpelier
Photograph by Shay Cochrane

INDEX